AF262919

NUESTRA SEÑORA DE LOS ÁNGELES

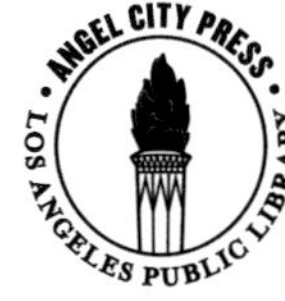

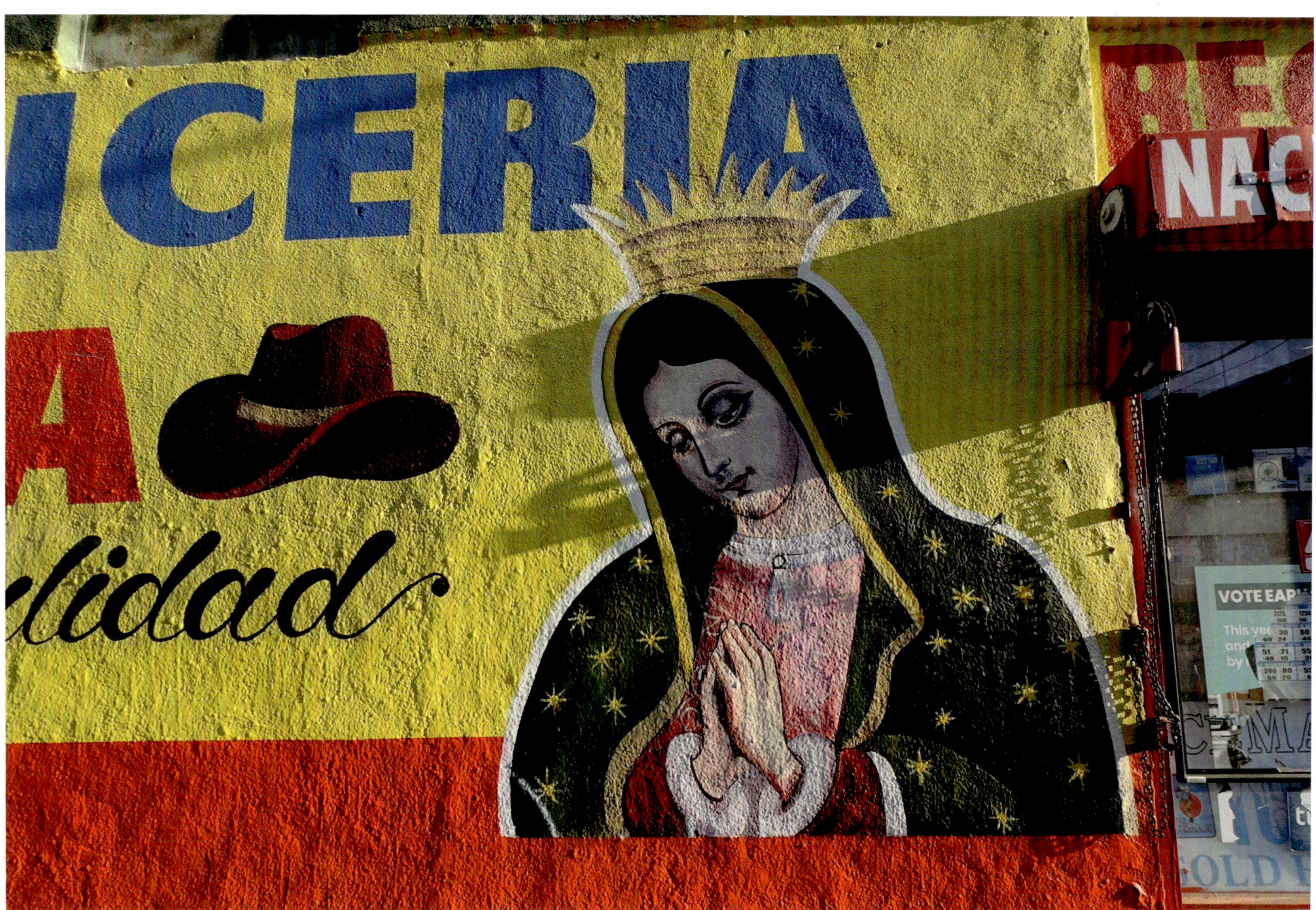
ICERIA
lidad
NAC
VOTE EAR
SOLD

SAM QUINONES

THE VIRGIN OF GUADALUPE
ON THE WALLS OF LOS ANGELES

OUR LADY OF THE ANGELS

米

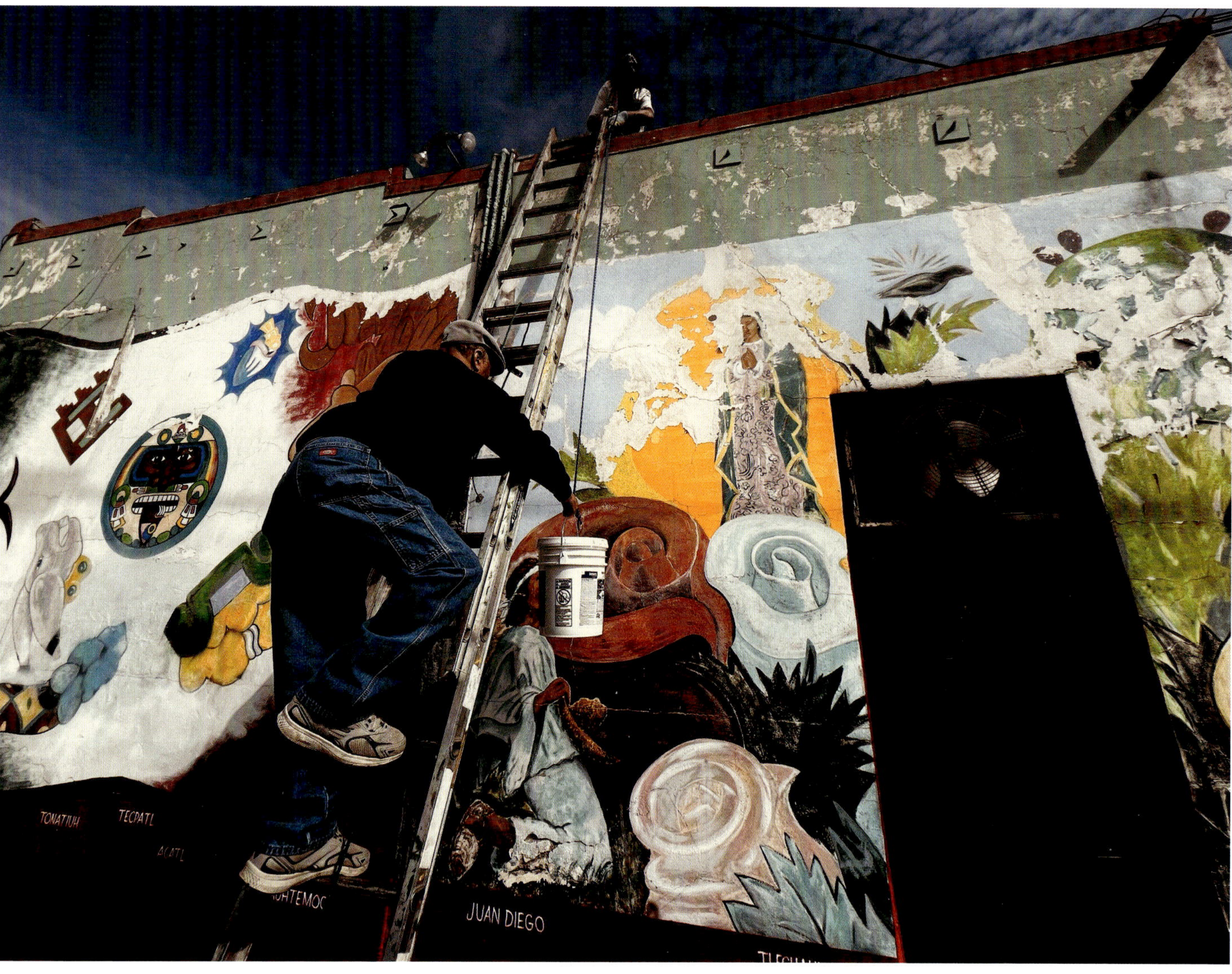
TONATIUH
TECPATL
ACATL
JUAN DIEGO

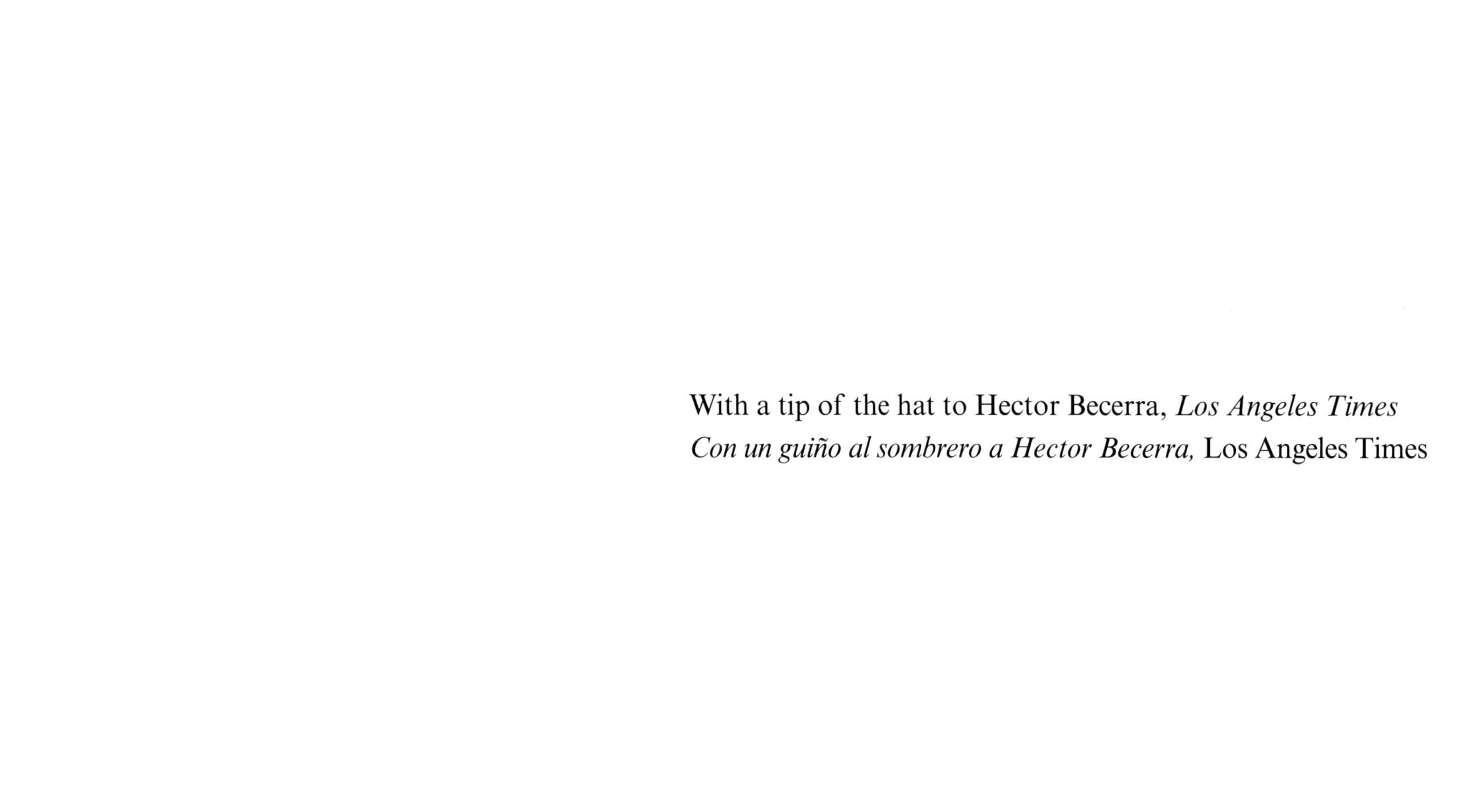

With a tip of the hat to Hector Becerra, *Los Angeles Times*

Con un guiño al sombrero a Hector Becerra, Los Angeles Times

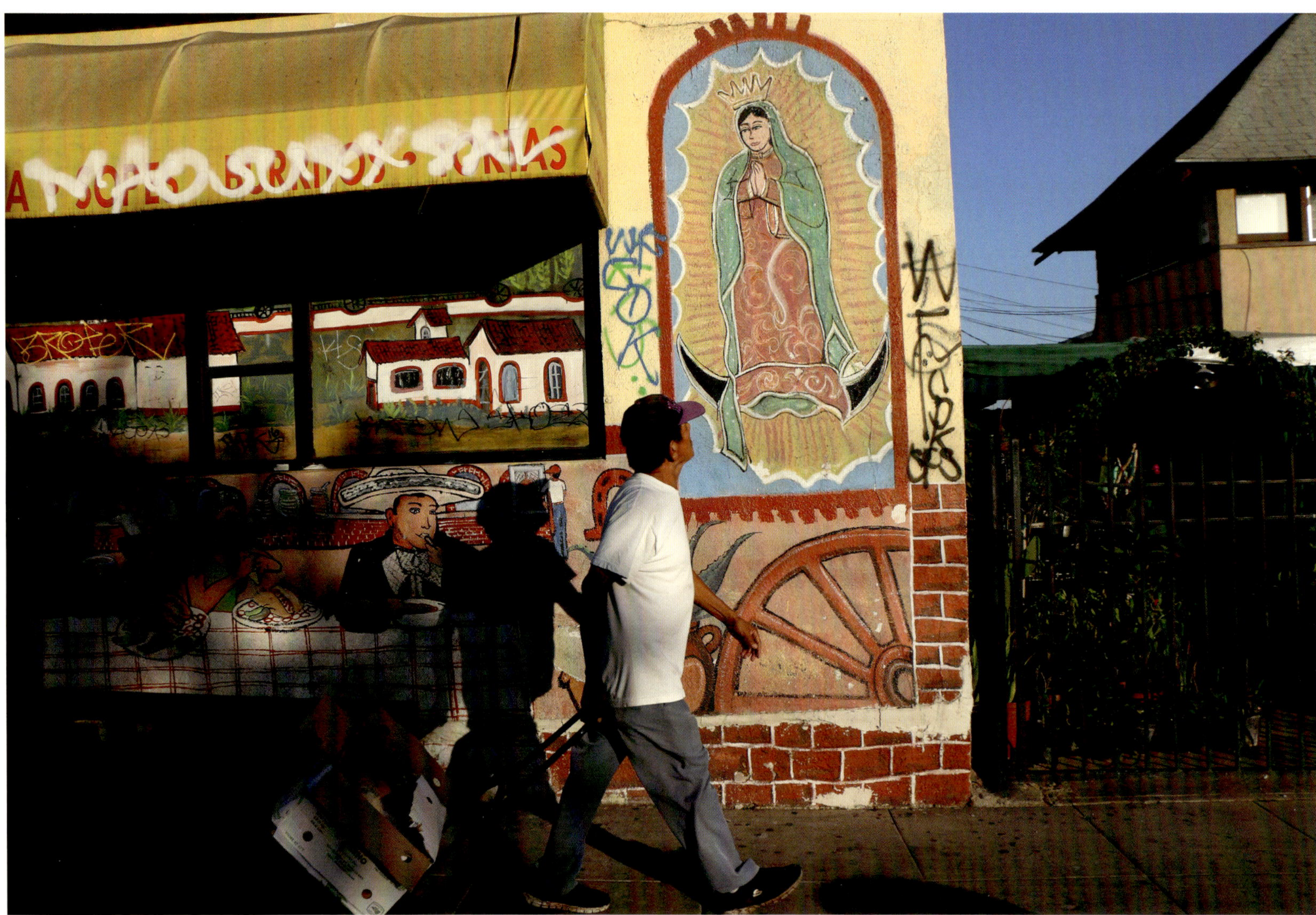

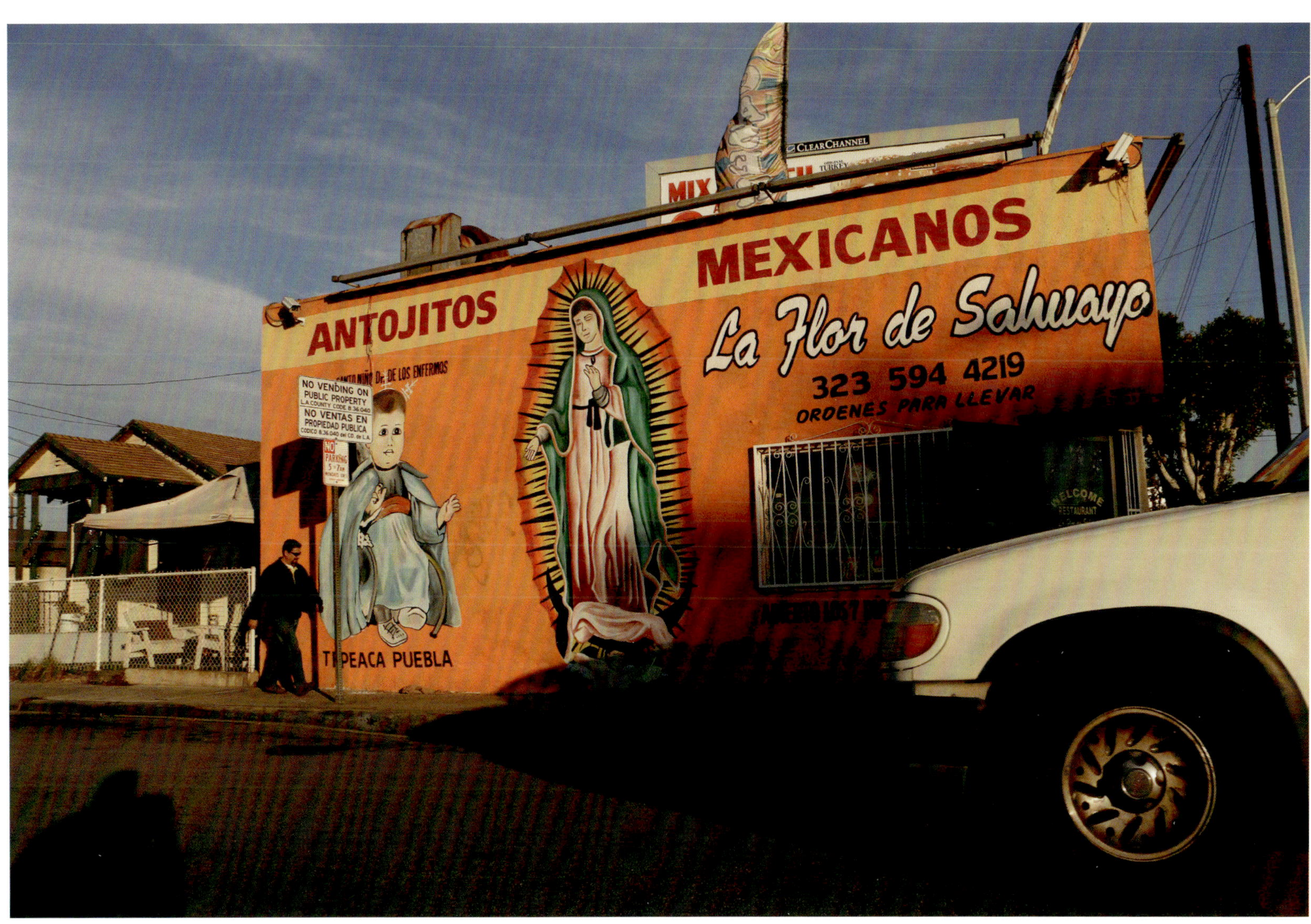
ANTOJITOS
MEXICANOS
La Flor de Sahuayo
323 594 4219
ORDENES PARA LLEVAR
DE LOS ENFERMOS
NO VENDING ON
PUBLIC PROPERTY
L.A. COUNTY CODE 8.36.040
NO VENTAS EN
PROPIEDAD PUBLICA
CODICO 8.36.040 del CO. de L.A.
NO
PARKING
PUEBLA
WELCOME
RESTAURANT
CLEARCHANNEL

FOREWORD BY GUSTAVO ARELLANO

She's *la guadalupana, la morenita*, Mother María, the Empress of the Americas.

Our Lady of Guadalupe. *Nuestra Señora de Guadalupe.*

Brown mother of Jesus. Crypto-Aztec goddess. Mexico's mami.

Muse of LA. Our Lady of Los Angeles.

The Virgin of Guadalupe has always been a part of my life, not just because I'm Catholic, but because of her ubiquity in mural form across Southern California. But not until Sam Quinones came out with this book did I ever think of Lupita as a personification of the American dream in all its beauty and peril.

In these pages, you will see Sam's shots of Guadalupe murals across Los Angeles, with his soaring prose telling the story of how she came to be so common and essential. What I love about Sam's take is that it shows how diverse She is. Artists imagine Her surrounded by flags, roses, Christmas lights. On top of a mountain, above a stream, behind a small altar where the faithful leave votive candles and flowers. Sometimes, she's just a small square in a wall; other times, her entire face takes up the side of the store. Her skin varies from the color of oat milk to a chocolate brown.

However she appears, Guadalupe is radiant. She is at home among Her children, waiting for us in our time of pain and rejoicement.

Though short, *Our Lady of the Angels* deserves to be on the Angeleno photo bookshelf alongside Ruscha, Shulman, Oriol, and other giants. It shows the city how it is: gritty, but proud, and willing to save any lost soul. All you need to do is listen to *Nuestra Señora de Los Angeles.*

— Gustavo Arellano is a columnist for the *Los Angeles Times* and owes a big chunk of his journalism career to reading Sam's wise words long ago on a bus bench in East Hollywood.

EL PREFACIO BY GUSTAVO ARELLANO

Ella es la guadalupana, la morenita, la madre María, la emperatriz de las Américas.

Nuestra Señora de Guadalupe.

Madre morena de Jesús. Cripto-diosa azteca. Mami de México.

Musa de Los Ángeles. Nuestra Señora de Los Ángeles.

La Virgen de Guadalupe siempre ha formado parte de mi vida, no por el hecho de ser católico, sino porque su ubicuidad en forma de murales con su imagen se encuentran por todo el sur de California. Pero no fue hasta que Sam Quinones publicó este libro que llegué a pensar en Lupita como una personificación del sueño americano en toda su belleza y peligro.

En estas páginas verás las fotos de Sam de los murales de Guadalupe por todo Los Ángeles, con su prosa elevada que cuenta la historia de cómo llegó a ser tan común y esencial. Lo que me encanta de la perspectiva de Sam es que muestra lo diversa que Ella es. Los artistas la imaginan rodeada de banderas, rosas y luces navideñas. En la cima de una montaña, sobre un arroyo, detrás de un pequeño altar donde los fieles dejan veladoras votivas y flores. A veces, ella es solo un pequeño cuadro en una pared; otras veces, su rostro entero ocupa el costado de una tienda. Su piel varía desde el color de la leche de avena hasta un café chocolate.

Sea como sea que aparezca, Guadalupe es radiante. Ella está en casa entre sus hijos, esperándonos en nuestros momentos de dolor y de júbilo.

Aunque es breve, Nuestra Señora de Los Ángeles merece estar en el estante fotográfico angelino junto a Ruscha, Shulman, Oriol y otros gigantes. Muestra a la ciudad como es: ruda, pero orgullosa y dispuesta a salvar a cualquier alma perdida. Todo lo que tienes que hacer es escuchar a Nuestra Señora de Los Ángeles.

— *Gustavo Arellano es un columnista del* Los Angeles Times *y le debe una gran parte de su carrera peri odística al haber leído las sabias palabras de Sam hace mucho tiempo, en una banca de autobús en el este de Hollywood.*

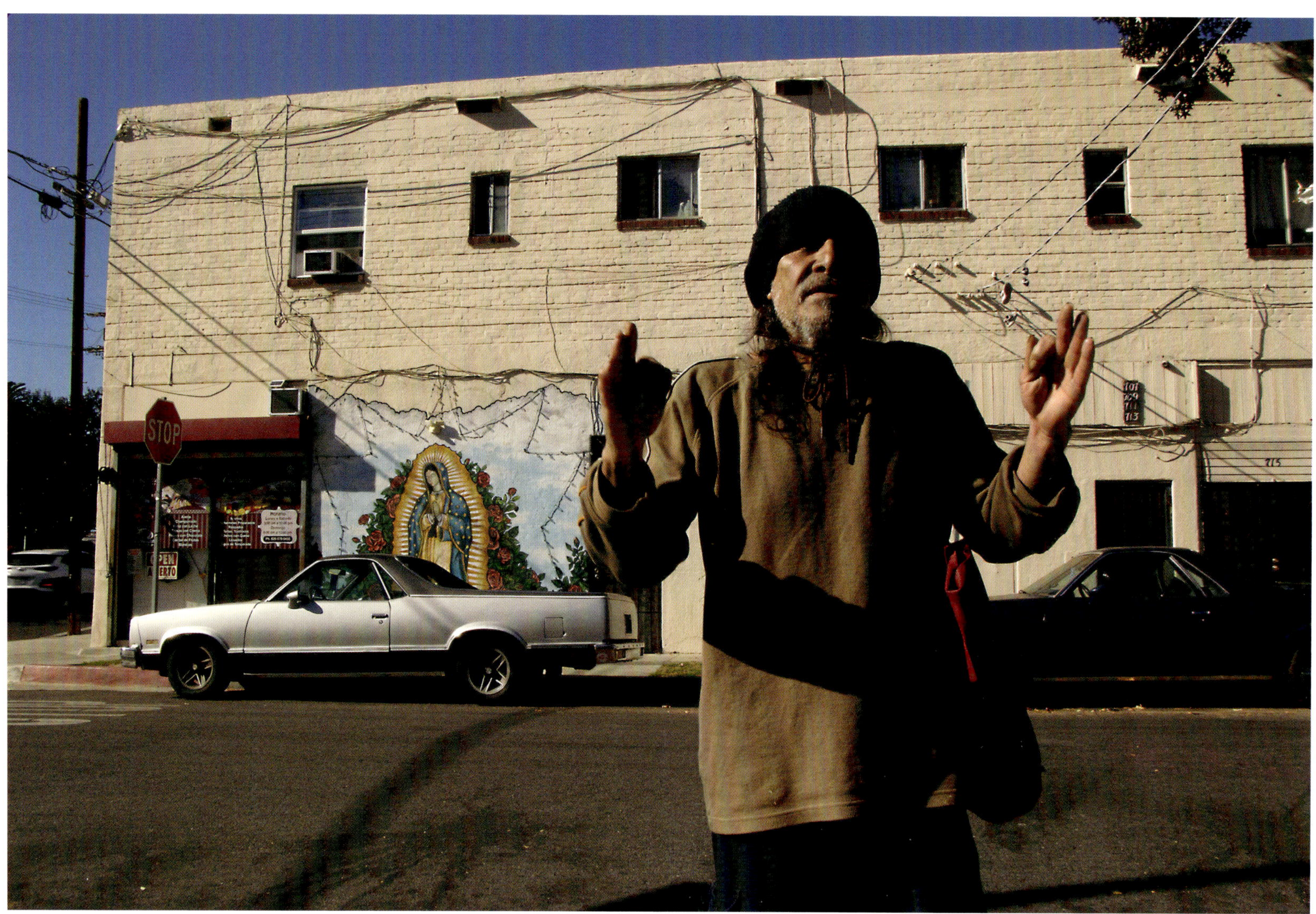
STOP
OPEN

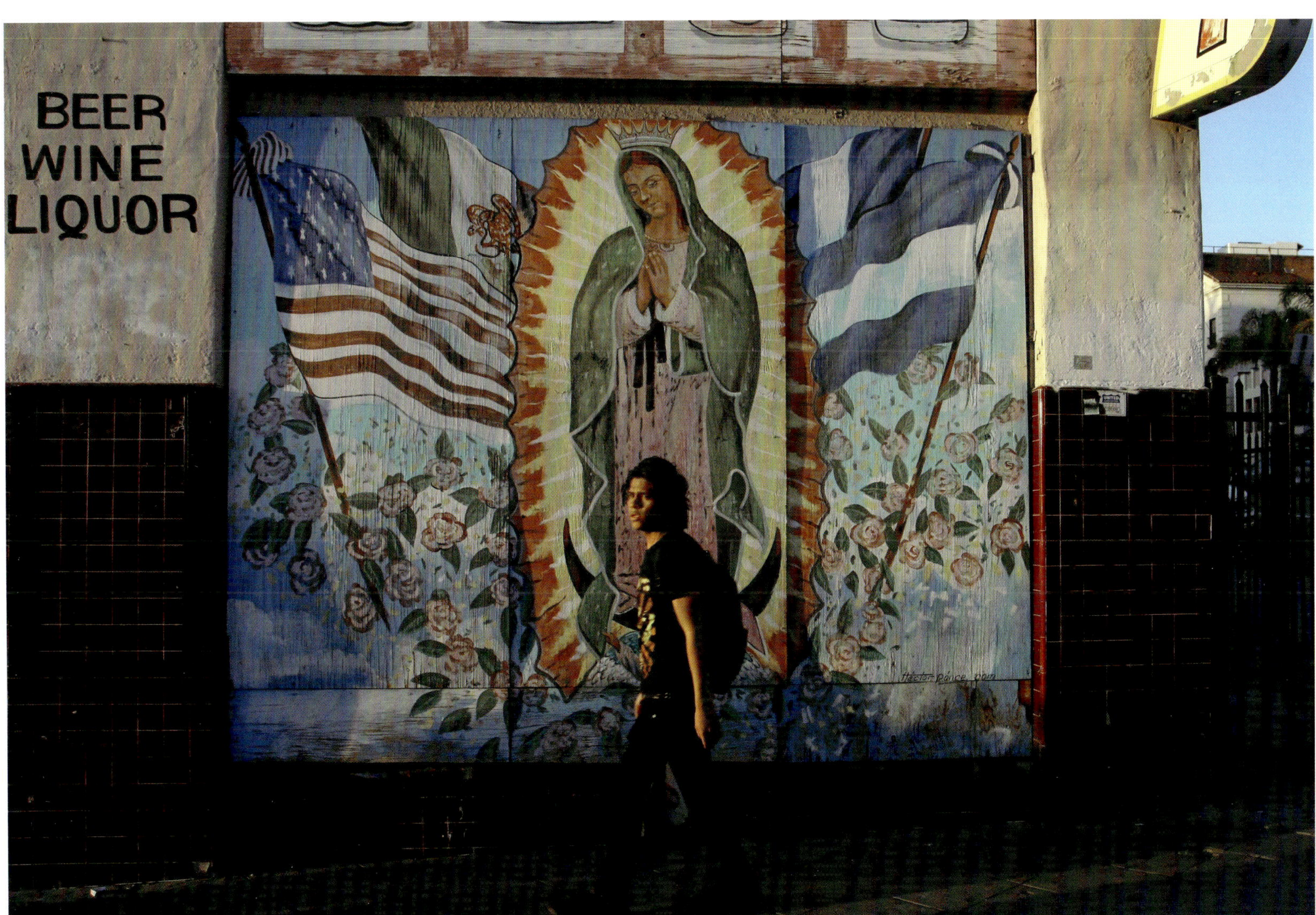
BEER
WINE
LIQUOR

ON DECEMBER 9, 1531, outside what is now Mexico City, on a hill where a shrine to Tonantzin, the Aztec goddess of fertility and earth, had been destroyed by the Spaniards, an apparition—a dark-skinned woman in simple dress—came to a man named Cuauhtlatoatzin, who had been baptized Juan Diego.

Speaking in his native tongue, she urged him to tell his bishop to build a church dedicated to her on the hill so she might become the patron of the people of this new world. She appeared to Juan Diego three more times.

"Am I not here, I who am your mother?" she asked him.

Finally, she told Juan Diego to gather roses from a barren hill and present them to the bishop. Suddenly, rose bushes appeared on the hill. Juan Diego brought them back to the bishop in his cloak. The roses fell to the floor before the bishop; an image of the Virgin appeared emblazoned on Juan Diego's cloak. As proof that she had a mother's power to soften the problems of the poor, she cured Juan Diego's uncle, who had been ill.

The day was December 12.

The Virgin of Guadalupe, as she became known, replaced Tonantzin, allowing the Aztecs, a civilization that had conquered many others, to coexist with their own conquerors and gain a protecting mother.

December 12 became the day of her veneration.

The Empress of the Americas, the Virgin became the intermediary for common people before God and a refuge for the vulnerable navigating a new world.

EN EL 9 DE DICIEMBRE, 1531, *afuera de lo que ahora es la Ciudad de México, en un cerro donde un santuario a Tonantzin, la diosa azteca de la tierra y fertilidad, había sido destrozado por los españoles, una aparición—una mujer morena de vestimenta sencilla—llegó a aparecer a un hombre llamado Cuauhtlatoatzin, quien había sido bautizado como Juan Diego.*

Ella le urgió en su idioma natal pedirle a su obispo que le construyera a ella una iglesia en el cerro para que se volviera la patrona del pueblo de este nuevo mundo. Ella se apareció tres veces más.

"¿No estoy aquí, yo que soy tu madre?" le preguntó.

Finalmente, mandó a Juan Diego a cortar rosas de un cerro árido y presentarlas al obispo. De repente, arbustos de rosas aparecieron sobre el cerro. Juan Diego las trajo en su manto al obispo. Las rosas cayeron al suelo ante el obispo; una imagen de la virgen apareció estampada sobre el manto de Juan Diego. Como prueba que tenía el poder de una madre de suavizar los problemas de los pobres, ella curó a un tío enfermo de Juan Diego.

El día fue el 12 de diciembre.

La Virgen de Guadalupe, como se le conoció, reemplazó a Tonantzin, permitiendo a los aztecas, una civilización que había conquistado a varias otras, hacer sus paces con sus propios conquistadores y ganar una madre protectora.

El 12 de diciembre es el día de su veneración

La Emperatriz de las Américas, ella se volvió la intermediaria para la gente humilde ante Dios y un refugio para los vulnerables que navegaban un nuevo mundo.

For years, gangs warred across Los Angeles. Children went to sleep with helicopters hovering above and their parents awoke the next day to shell casings in the street.

Por años, las pandillas batallaron a lo largo de Los Ángeles. Los niños se dormían con helicópteros sobrevolando y sus padres se levantaban al día siguiente con casquillos en la calle.

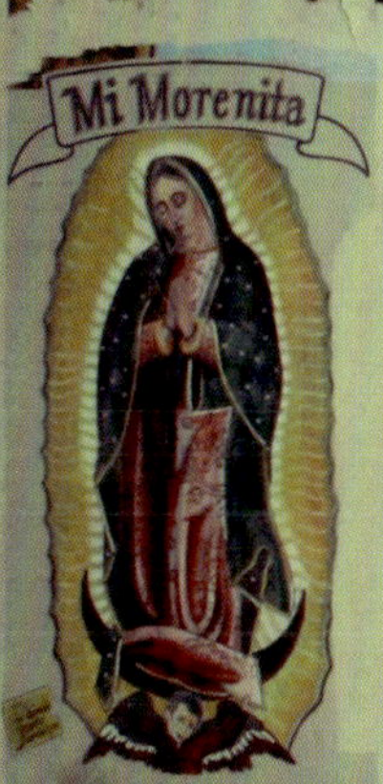
RINO'S MEAT MARKET
Mi Morenita

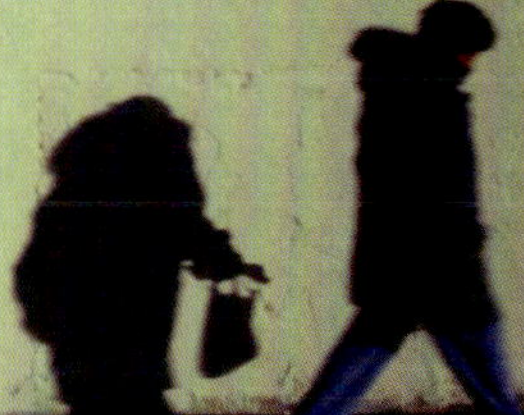

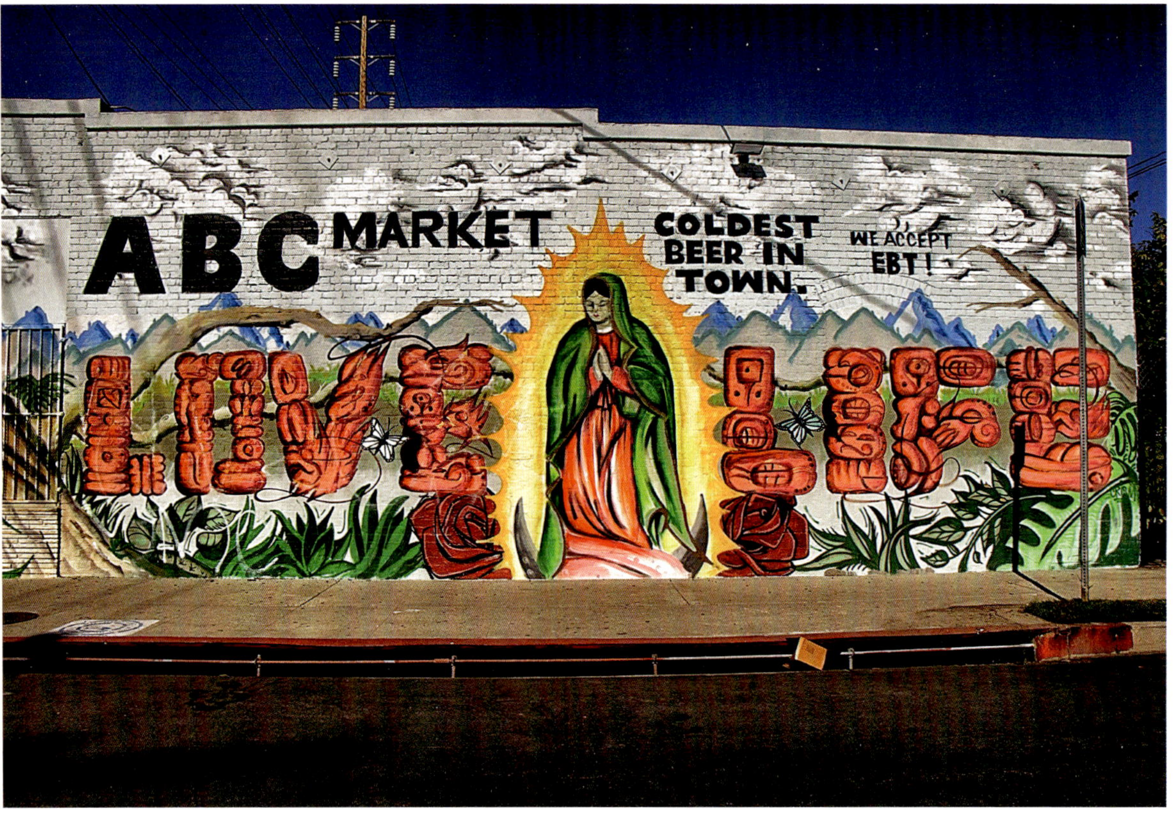
ABC MARKET
COLDEST BEER IN TOWN.
WE ACCEPT EBT!
LOVE LIFE

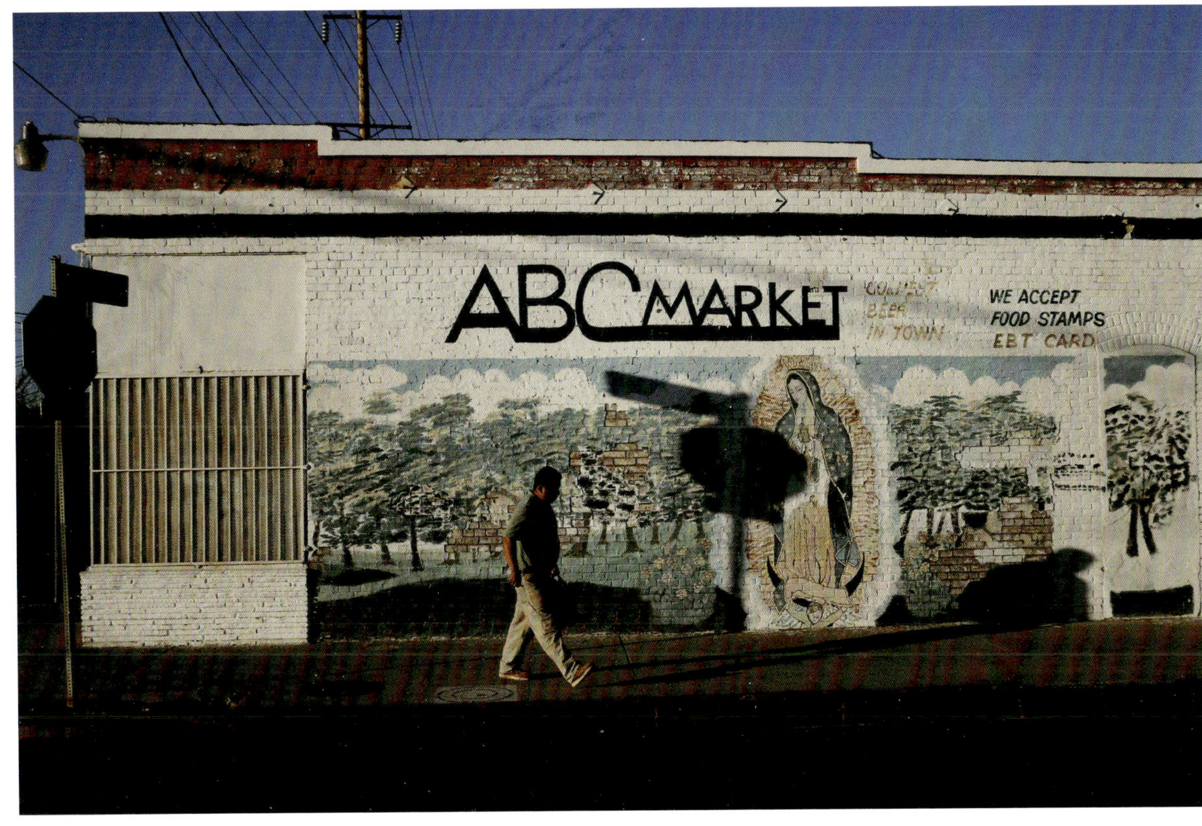

Graffiti was the most common form of degradation that gangs visited upon their neighborhoods.

El graffiti era la degradación más común que las pandillas impusieron sobre sus colonias.

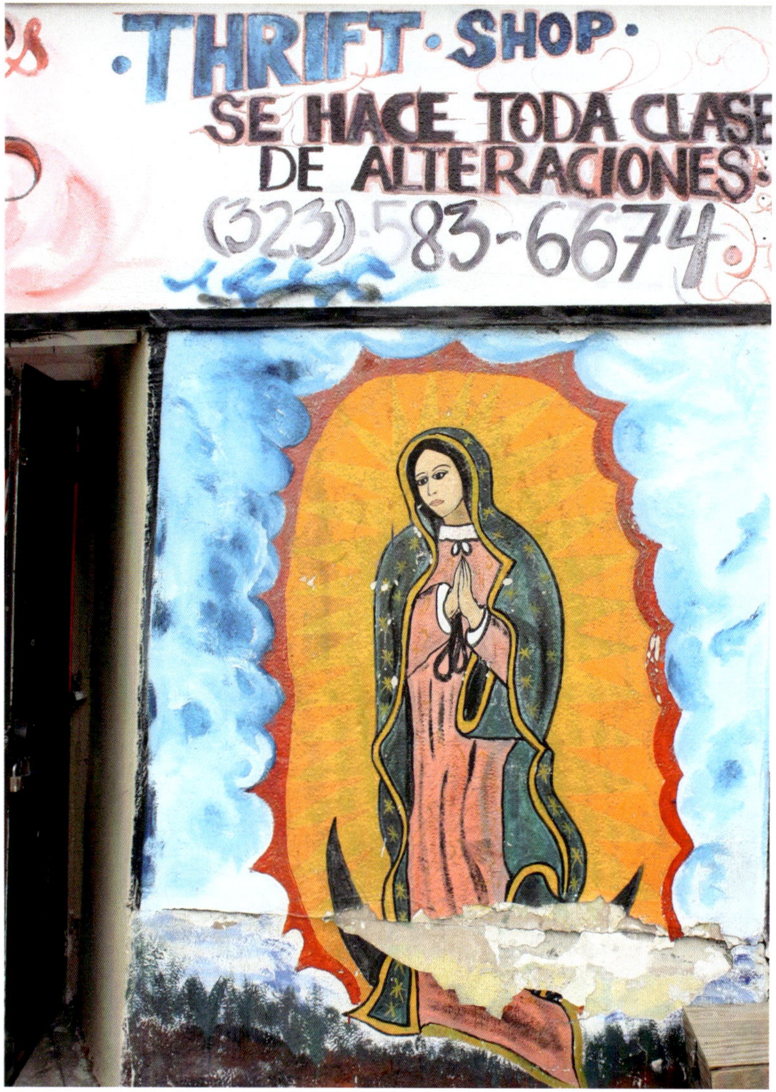

THRIFT · SHOP
SE HACE TODA CLASE
DE ALTERACIONES
(323) 583-6674

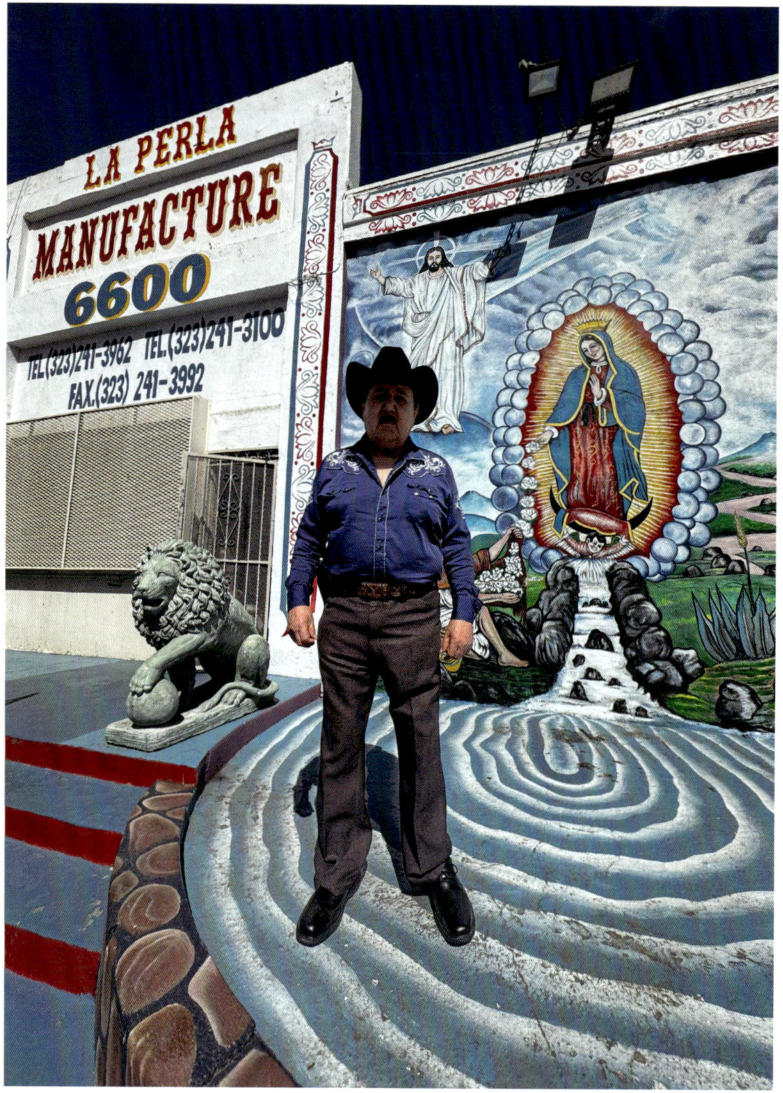

LA PERLA
MANUFACTURE
6600
TEL.(323)241-3962 TEL.(323)241-3100
FAX.(323) 241-3992

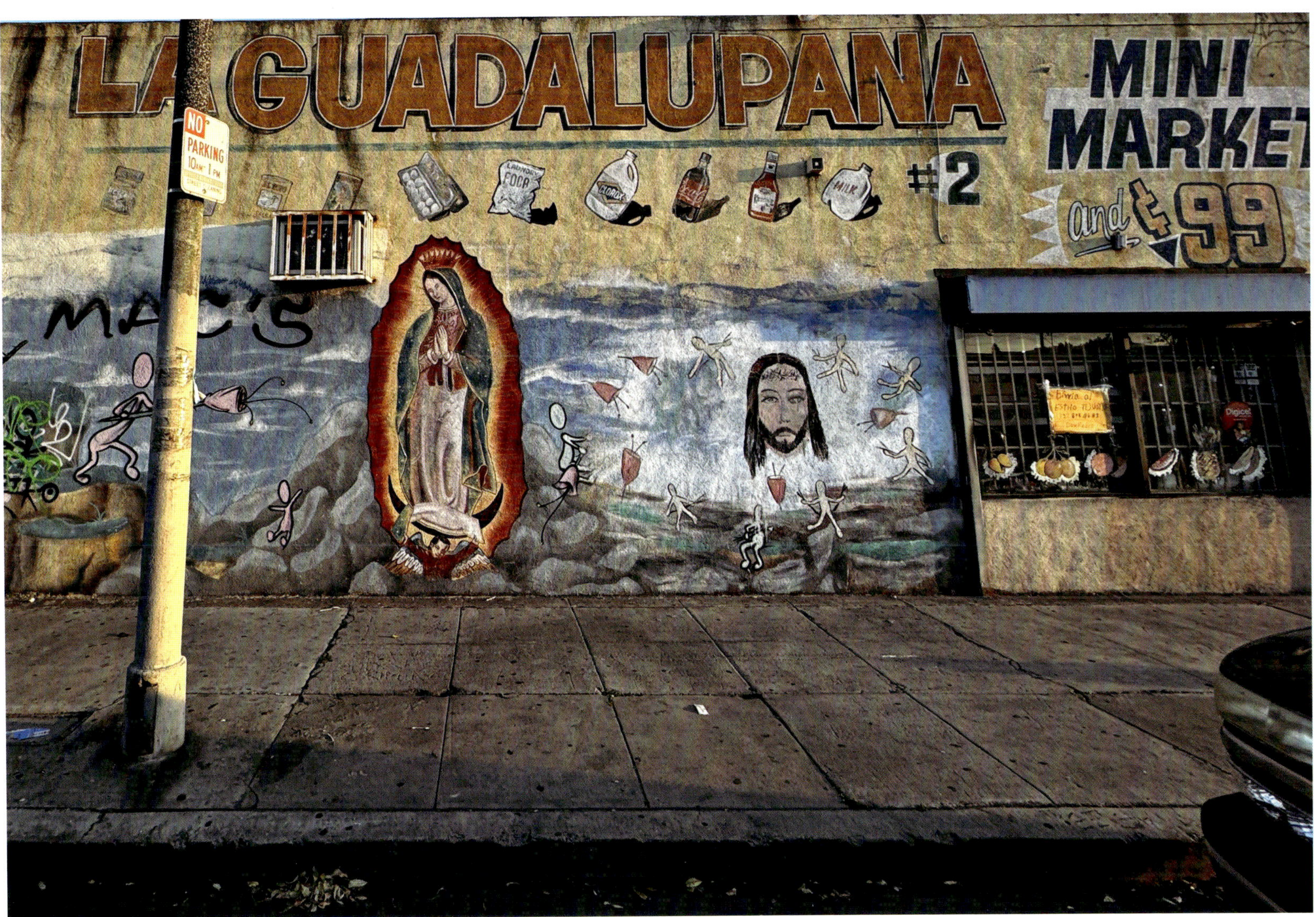

LA GUADALUPANA
MINI
MARKET
#2
and ¢99
NO PARKING
MAC'S

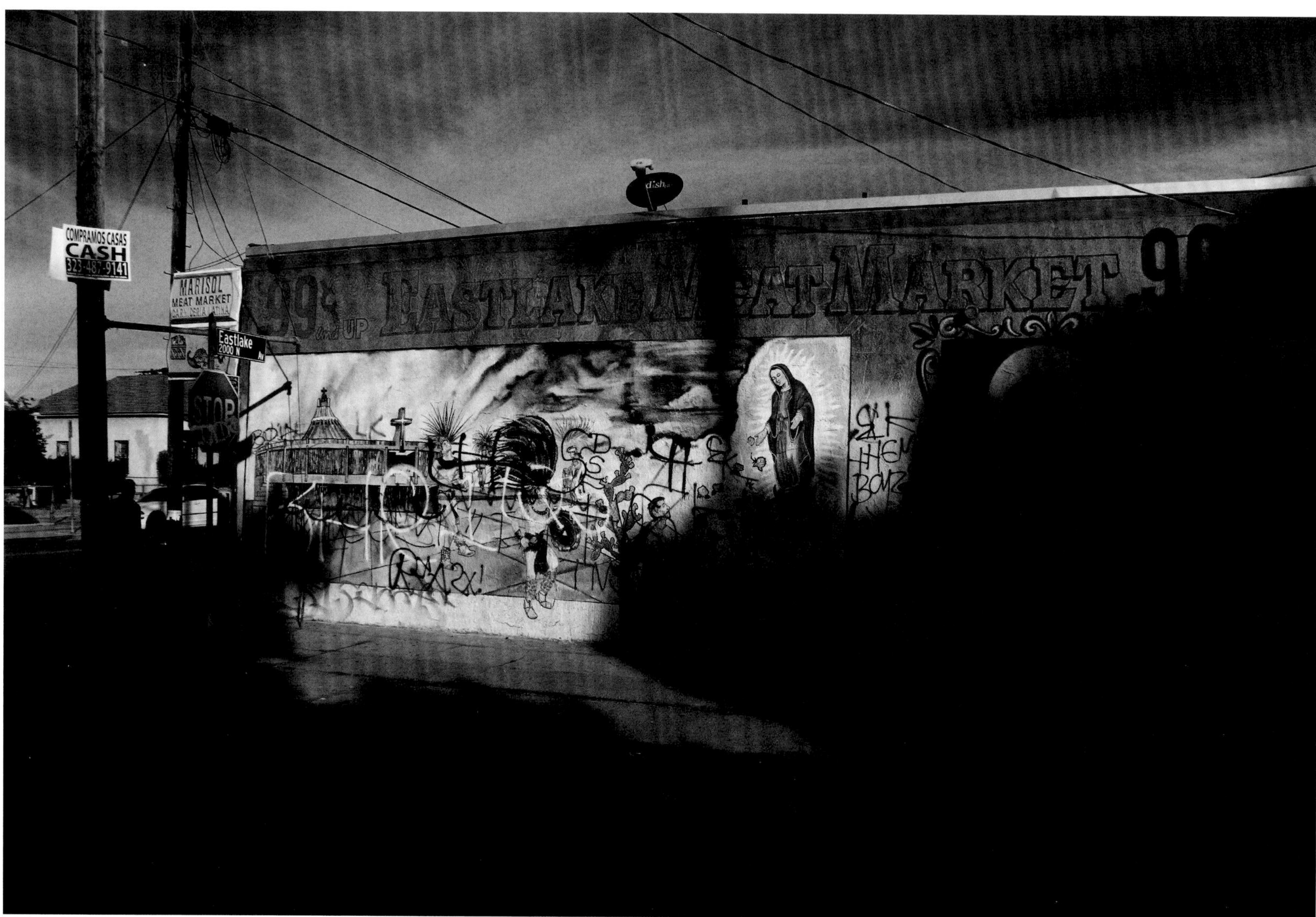
COMPRAMOS CASAS
CASH
323-487-9141
MARISOL
MEAT MARKET
Eastlake
2000 N
Av
STOP
dish
99¢ and UP
EASTLAKE
MARKET

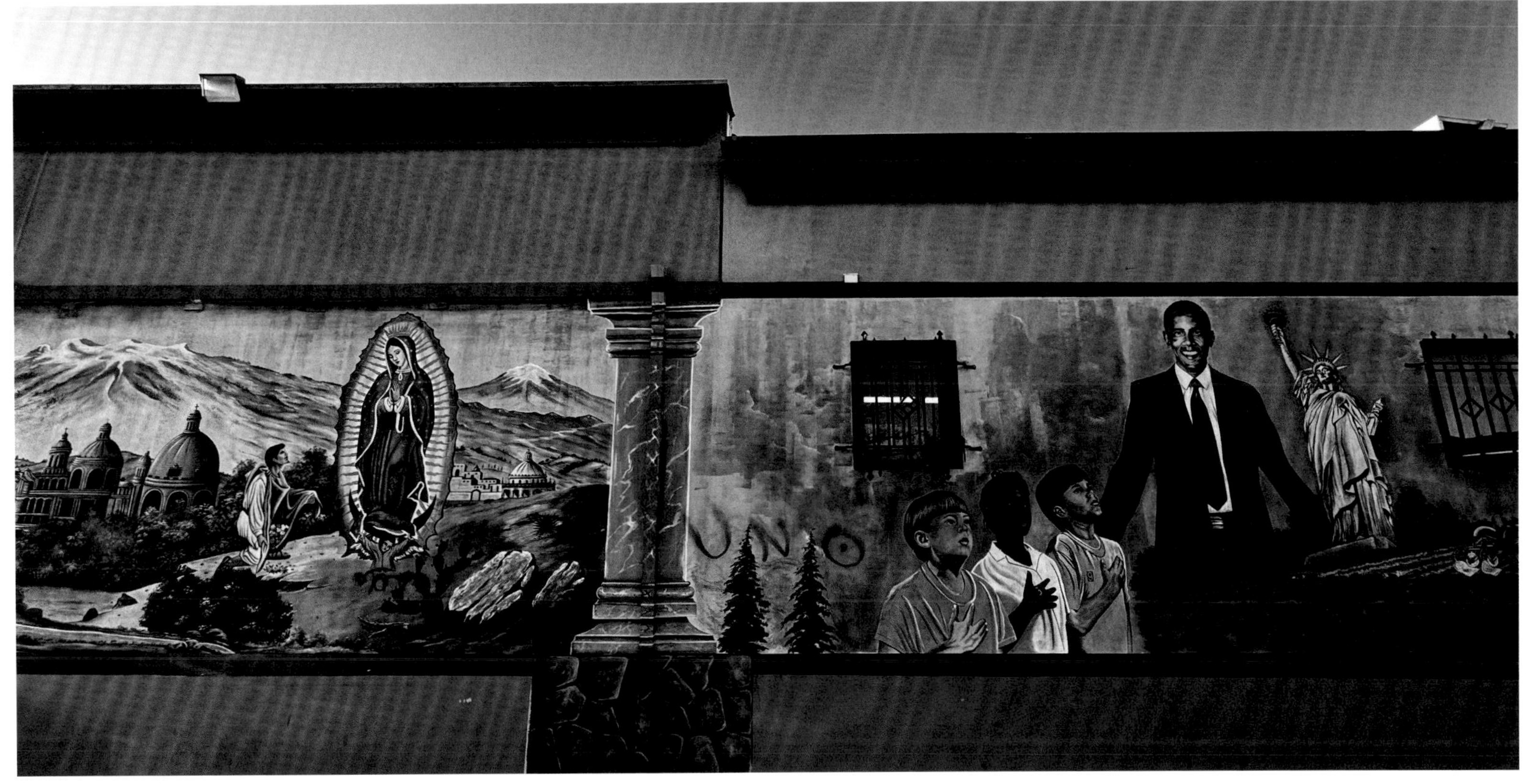

It spread across the walls of houses and small businesses belonging to working people who could least afford its torment.

Apareció en paredes de casas y pequeños negocios cuyos dueños eran gente trabajadora quienes menos podían aguantar su tormento.

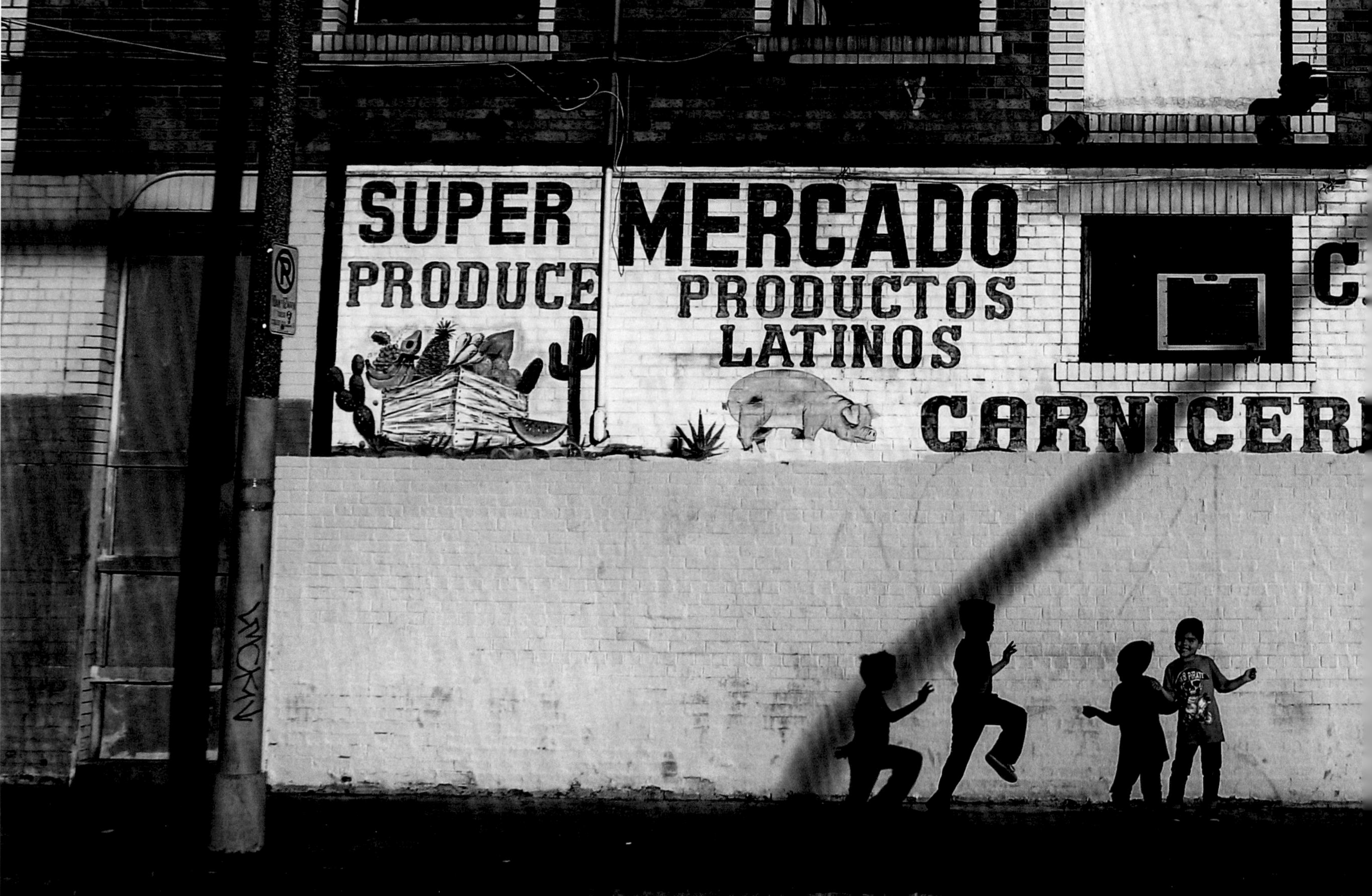
SUPER MERCADO
PRODUCE
PRODUCTOS
LATINOS
CARNICER

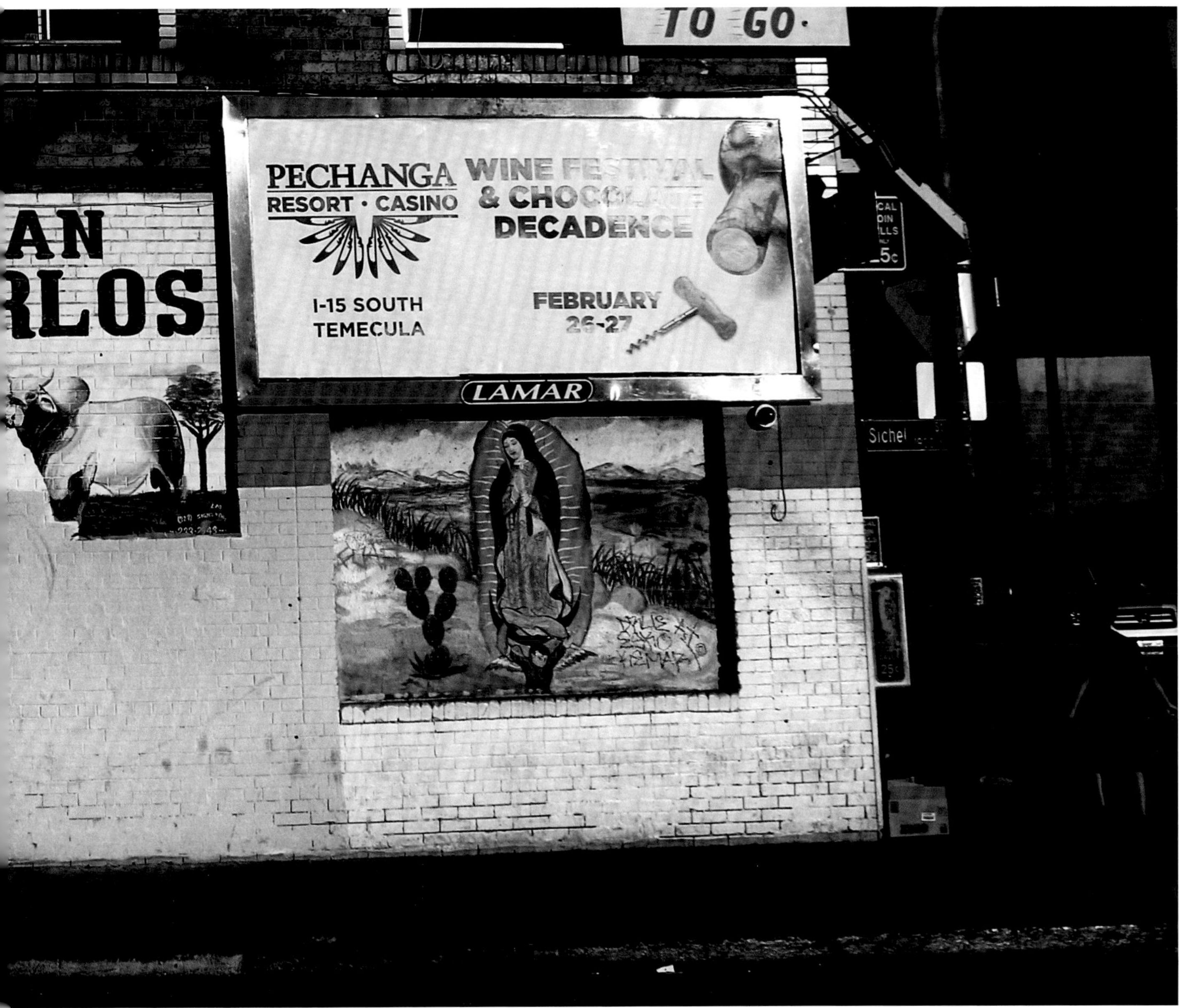
TO GO·
PECHANGA
RESORT · CASINO
WINE FESTIVAL
& CHOCOLATE
DECADENCE
I-15 SOUTH
TEMECULA
FEBRUARY
26-27
LAMAR
AN
RLOS
Sichel

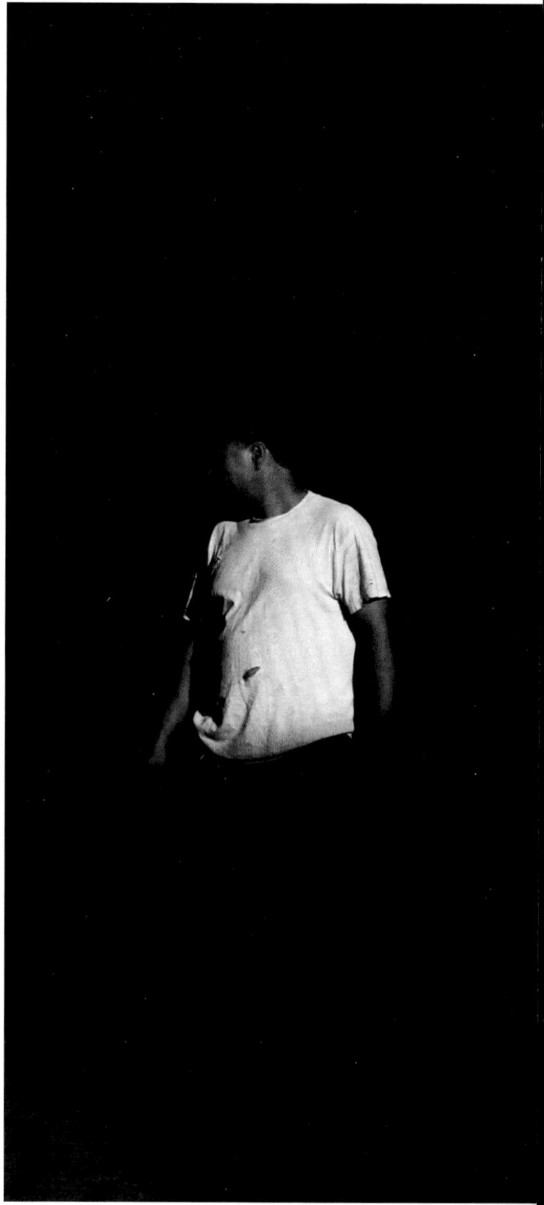

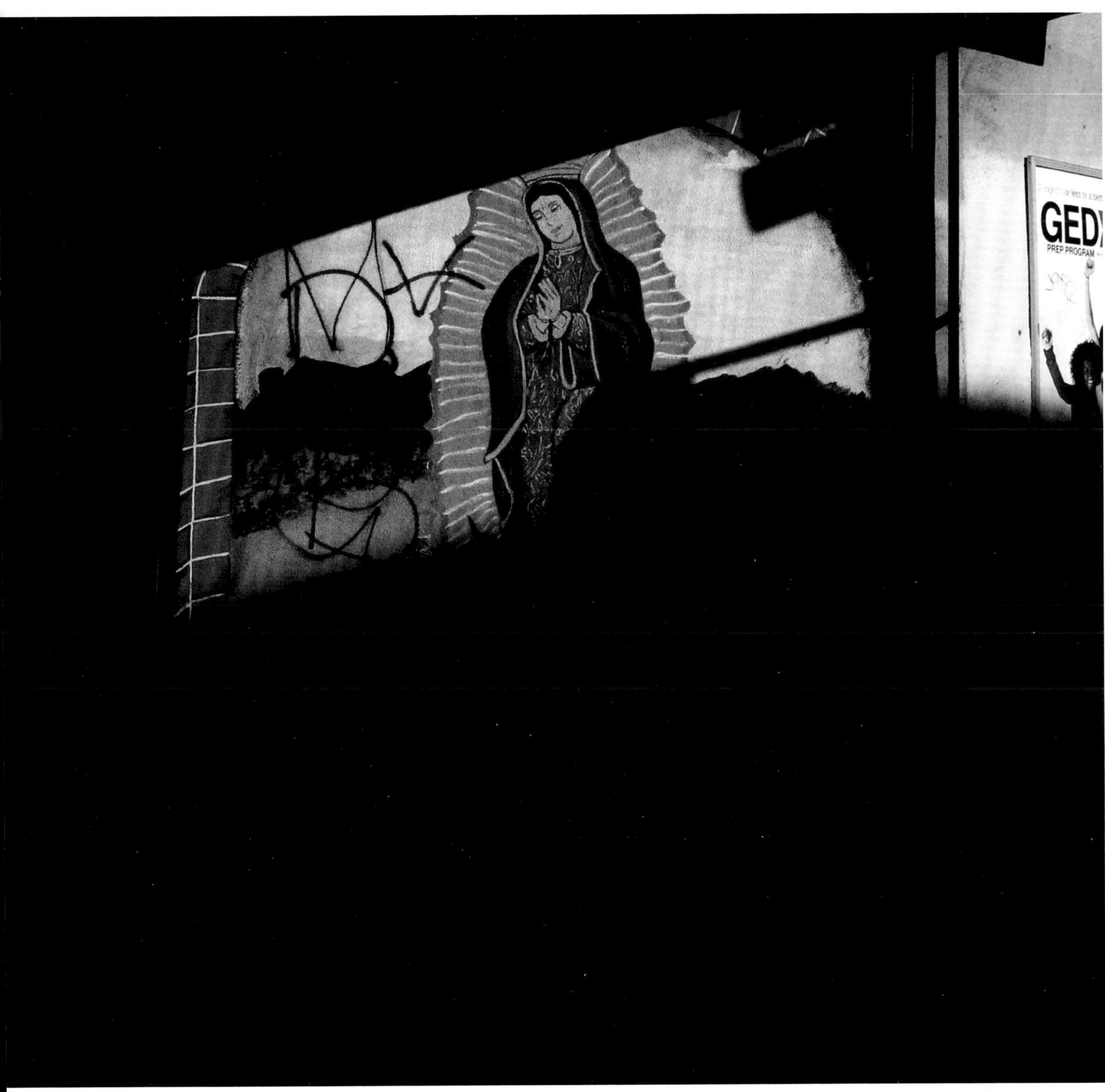
GED
PREP PROGRAM

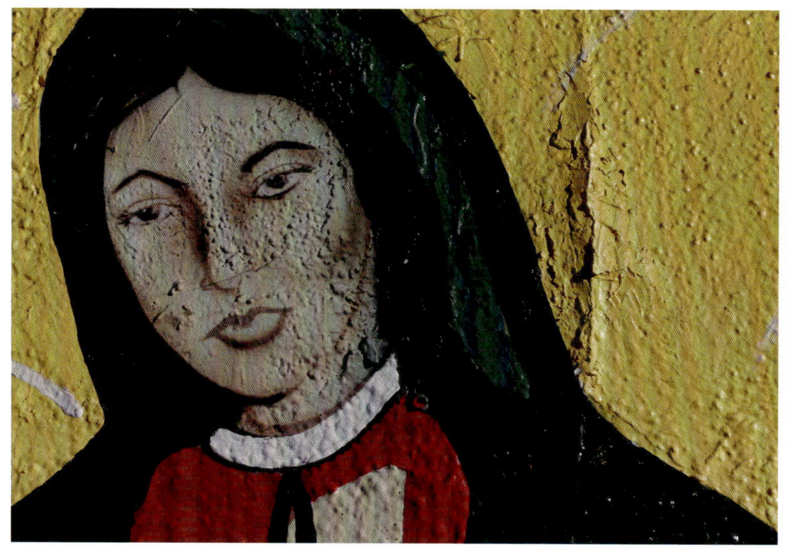

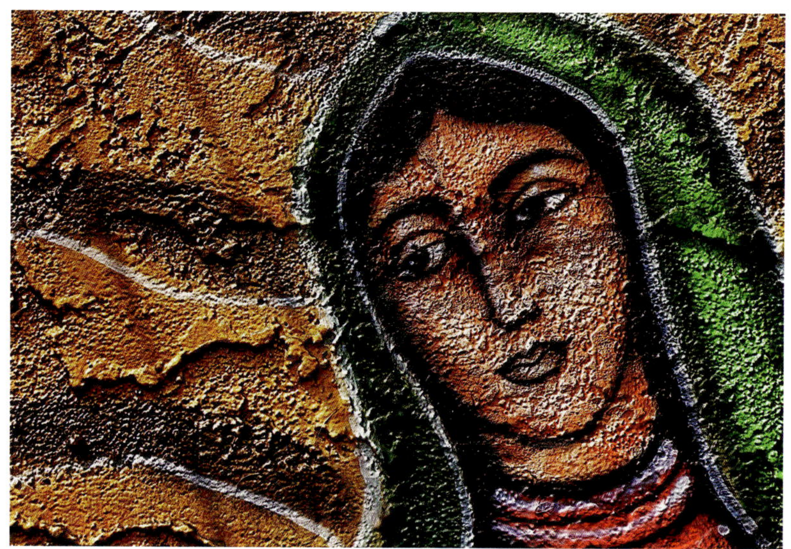

In Mexico centuries earlier, the Virgin of Guadalupe had appeared to a people adjusting to a new world before them. She was their Sacred Mother, offering tenderness and love, and a personal connection to God.

En México, siglos antes, la Virgen de Guadalupe había aparecido ante un pueblo que se ajustaba a un Nuevo Mundo. Ella era su Madre Sagrada, ofreciéndoles ternura y amor y una conexión personal con Dios.

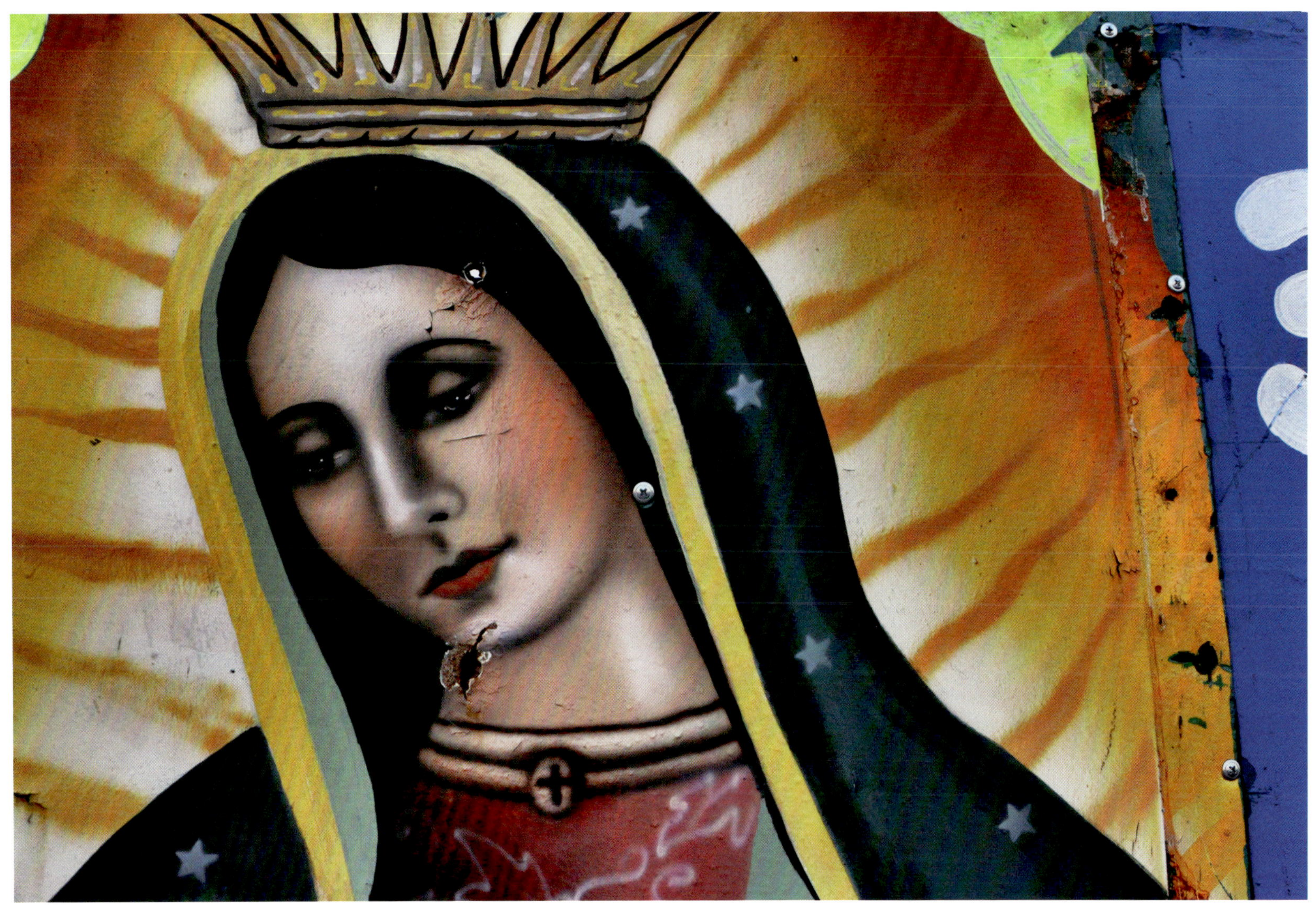

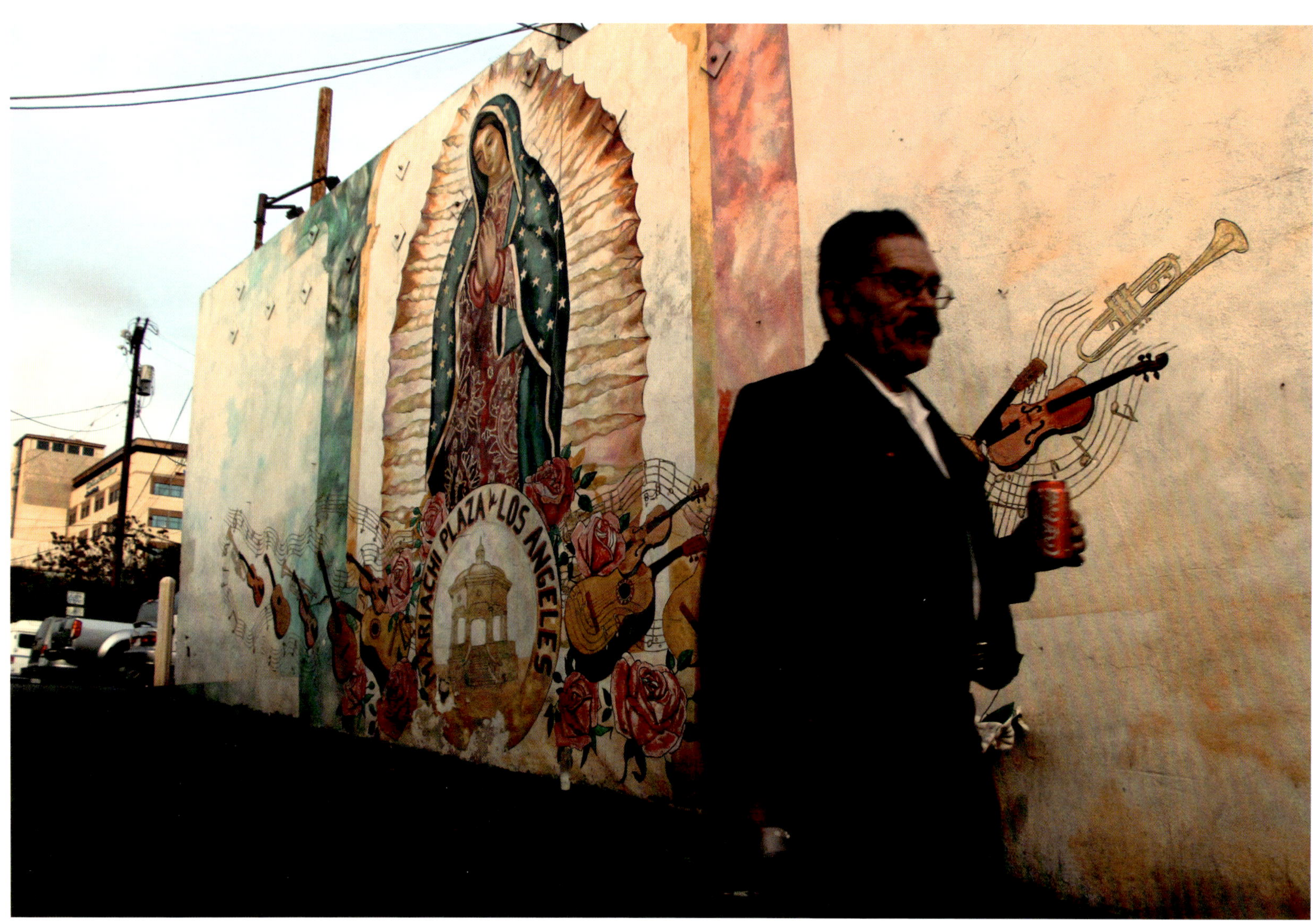
MARIACHI PLAZA LOS ANGELES

Faith in her came to dwell most deeply beyond the churches, on hard streets among defenseless people, who appealed to her directly, often without a priest, bishop, or an archbishop in between.

La fe en ella vivió más profundamente más allá de las iglesias, en calles duras entre gente indefensa, quienes recurrían a ella directamente, sin un sacerdote, obispo, o arzobispo como intermediario.

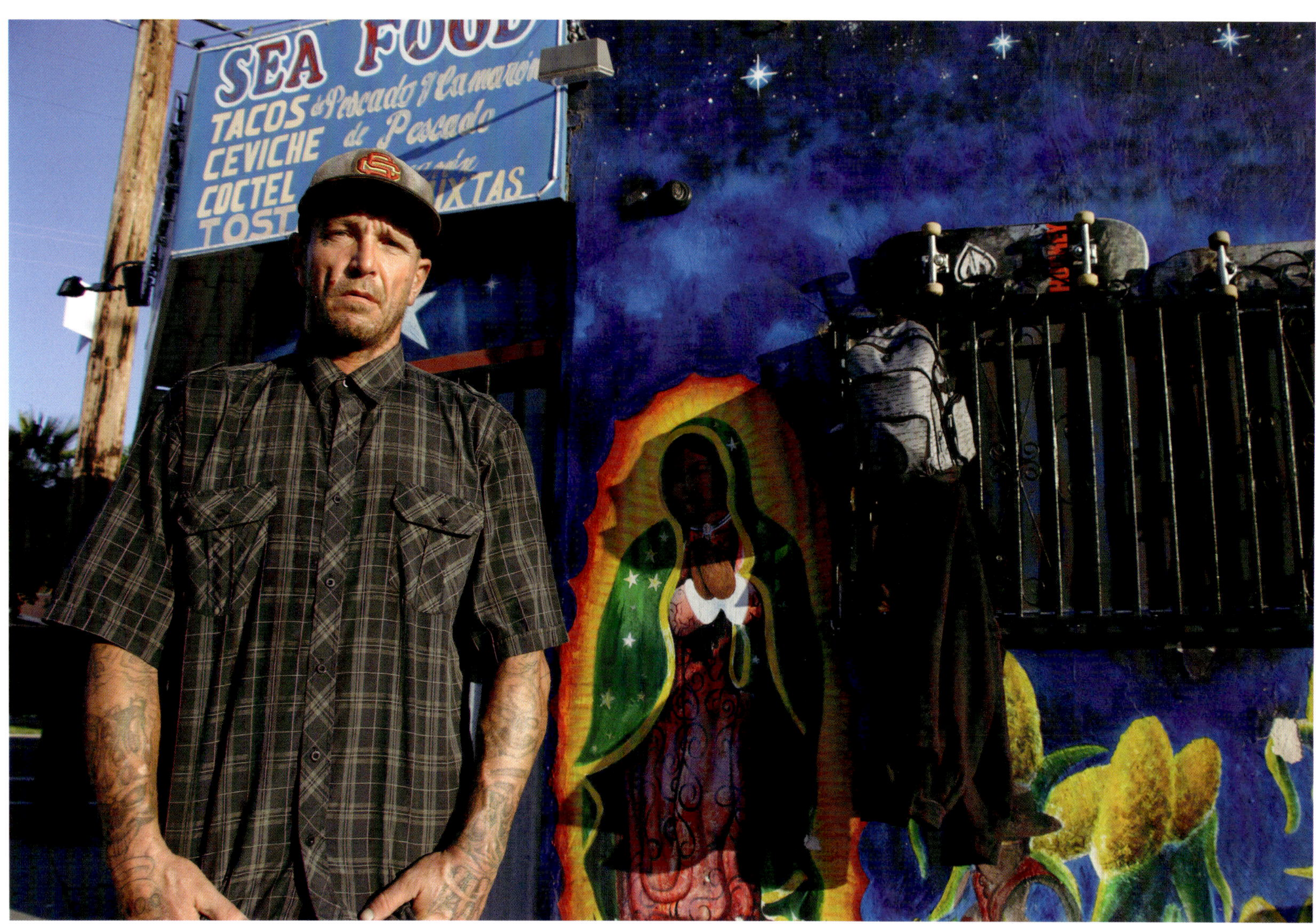
SEA FOOD
TACOS de Pescado y Camarón
CEVICHE de Pescado
COCTEL

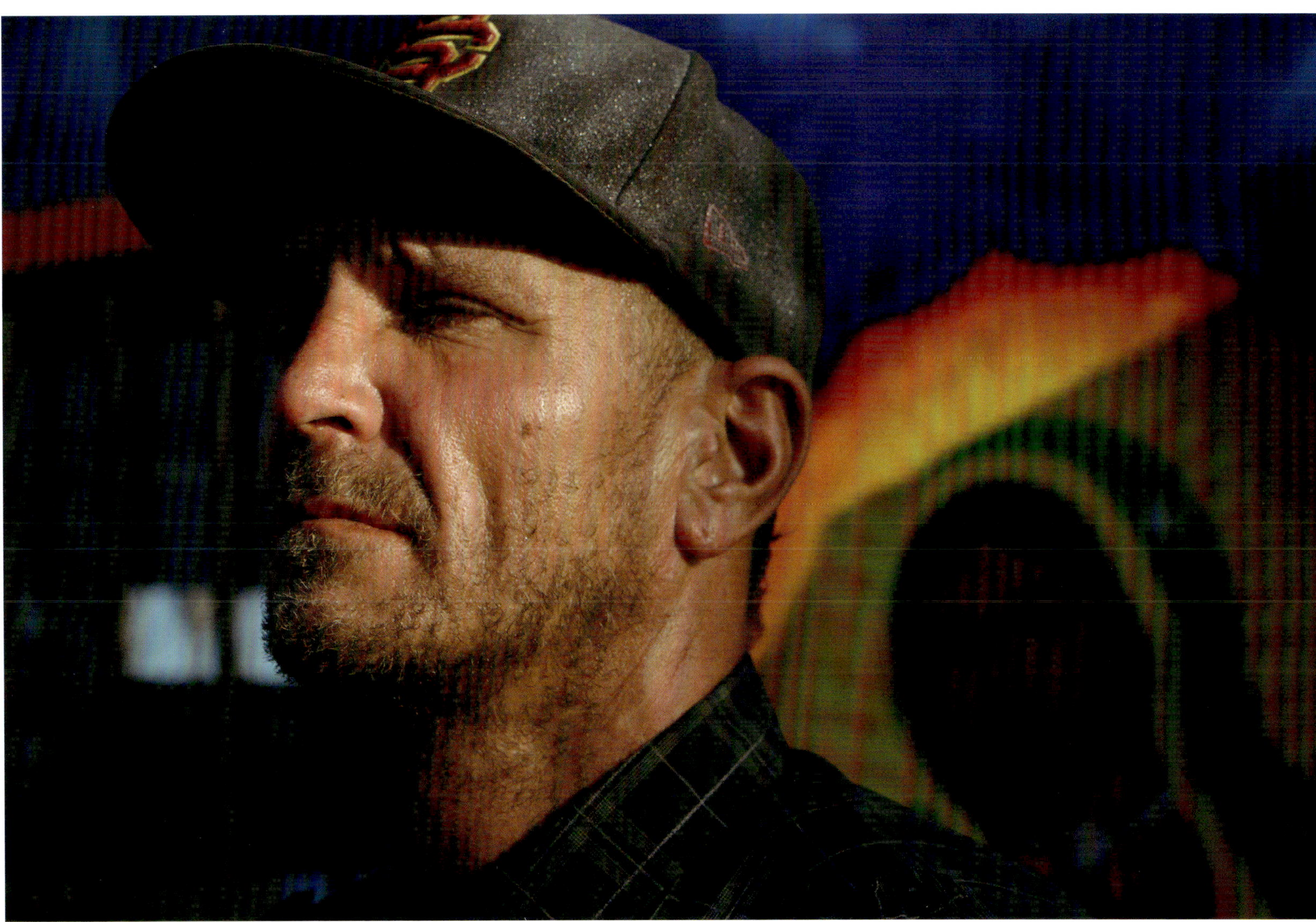

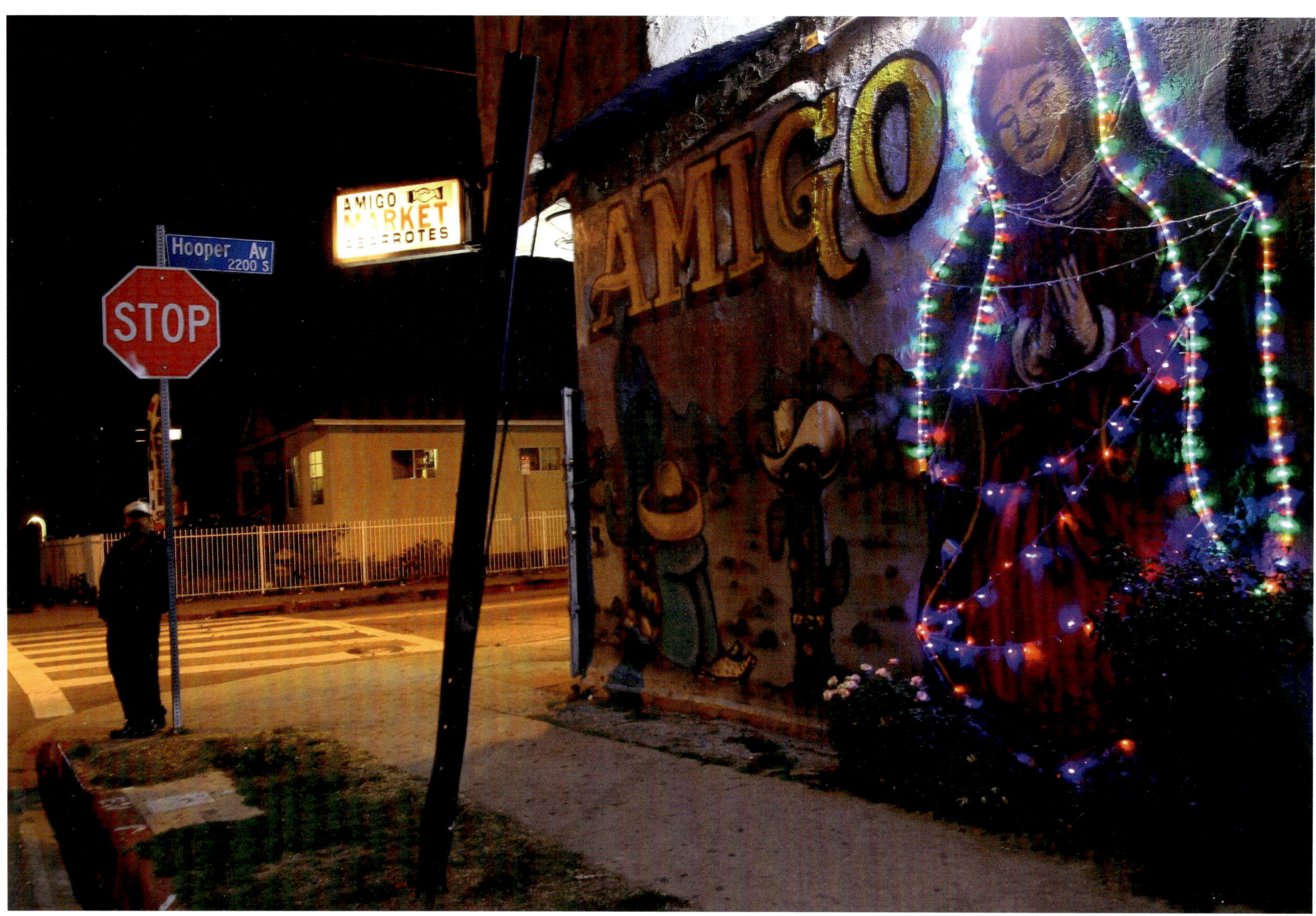
Hooper Av
2200 S
STOP
AMIGO
MARKET
AMIGO

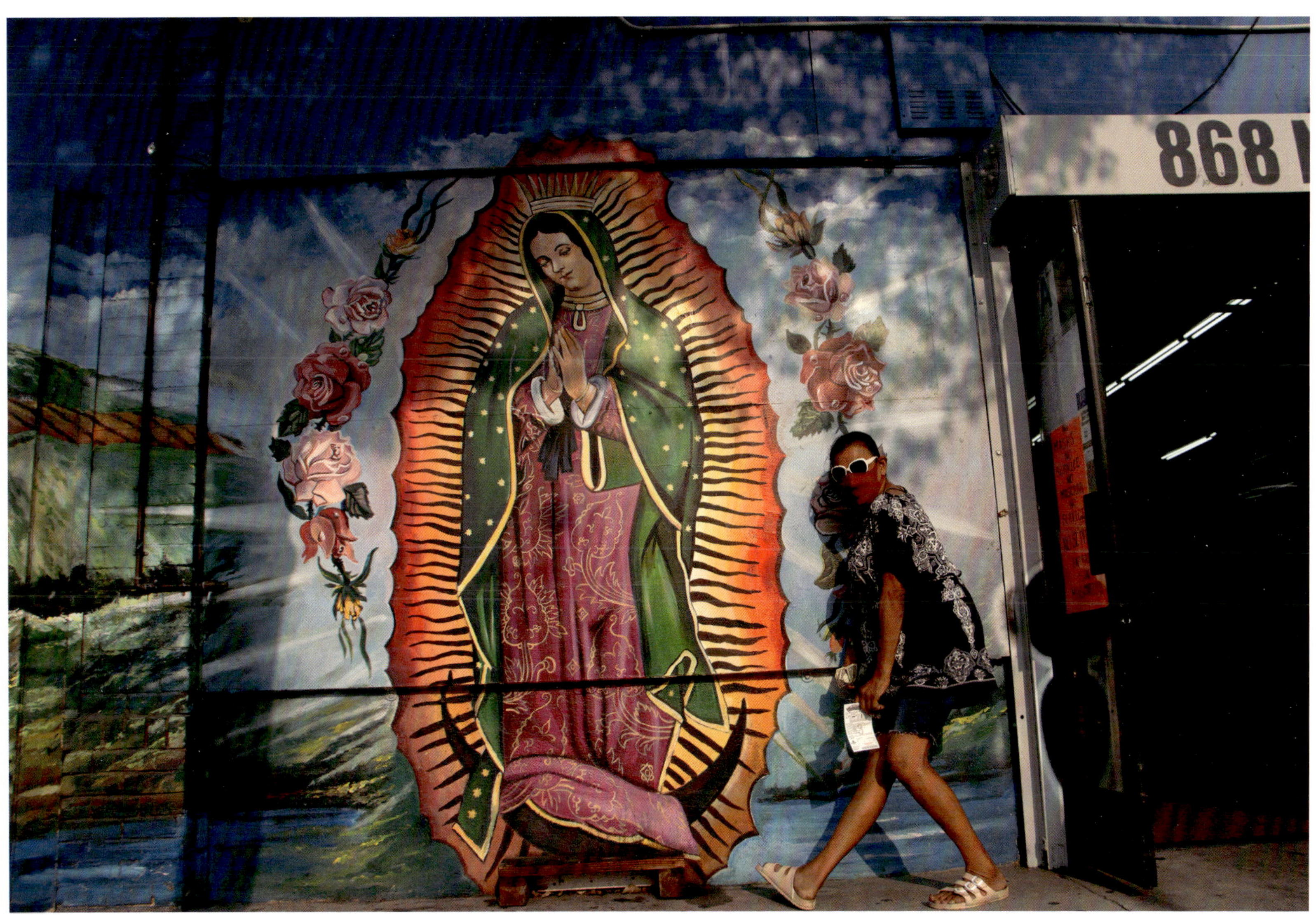
868

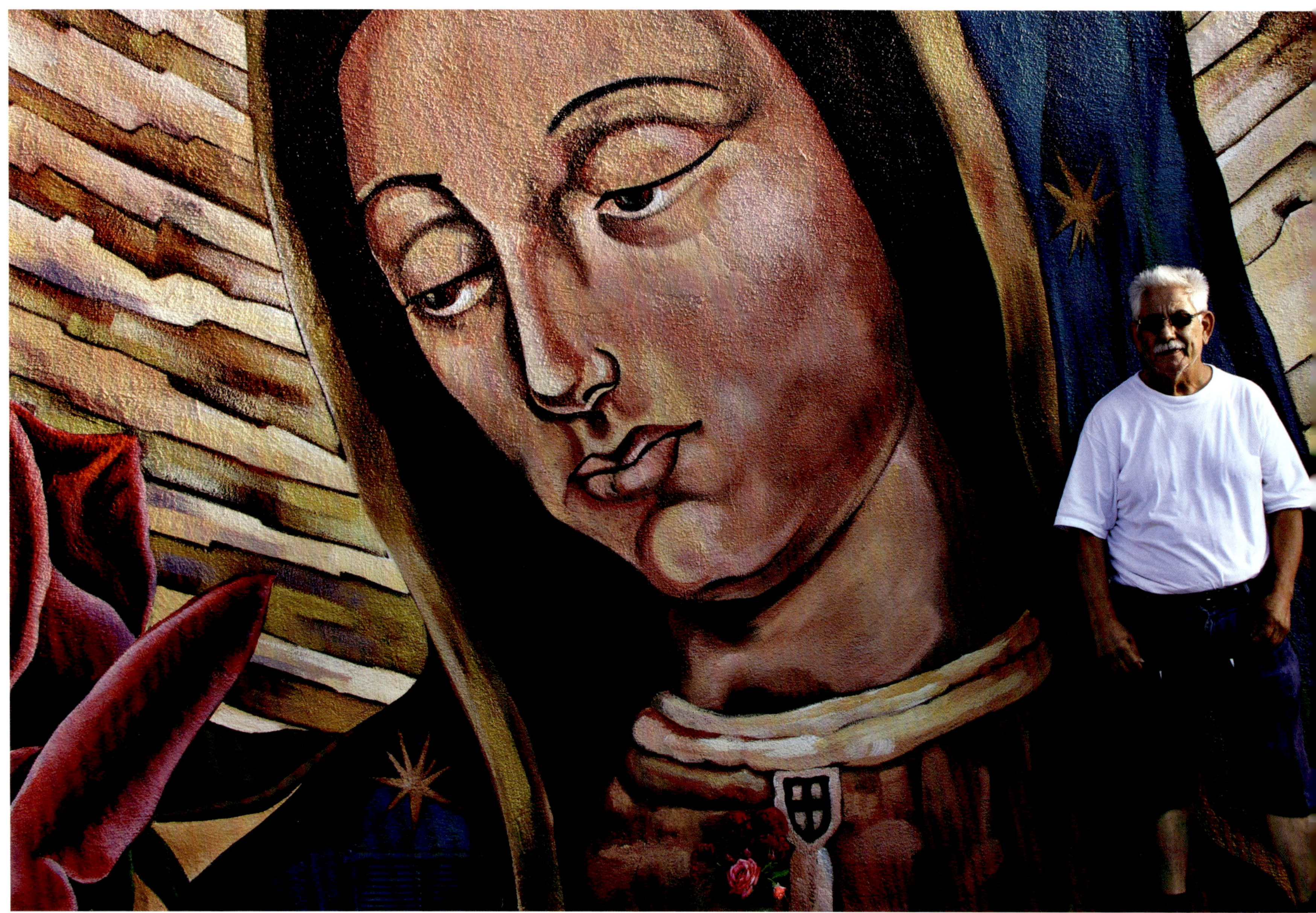

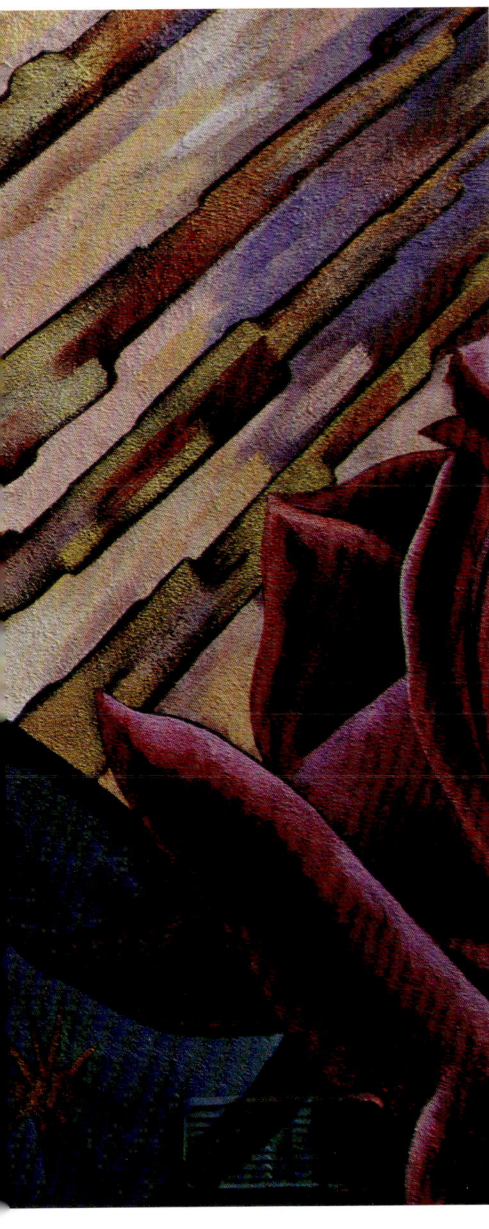

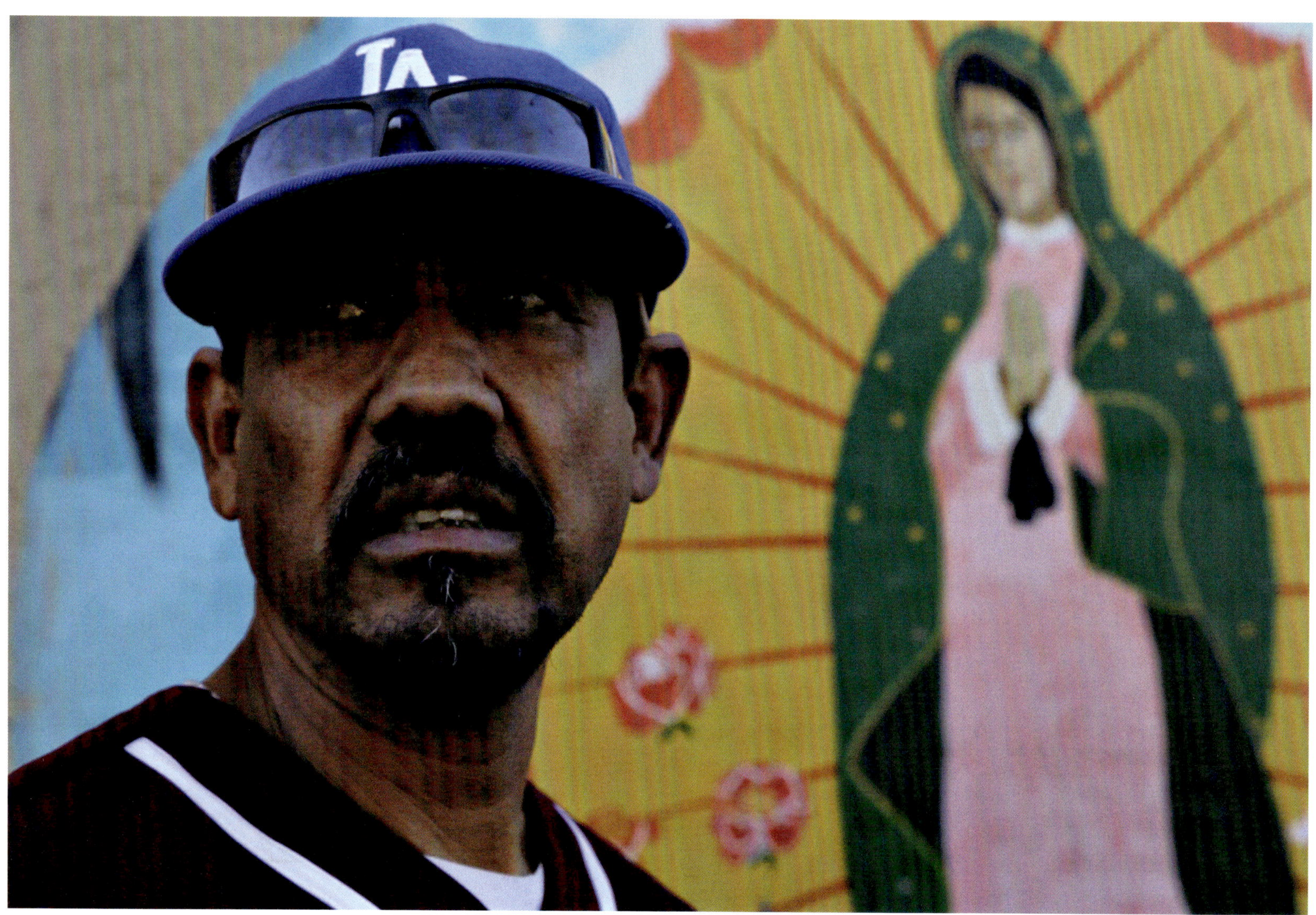
LA

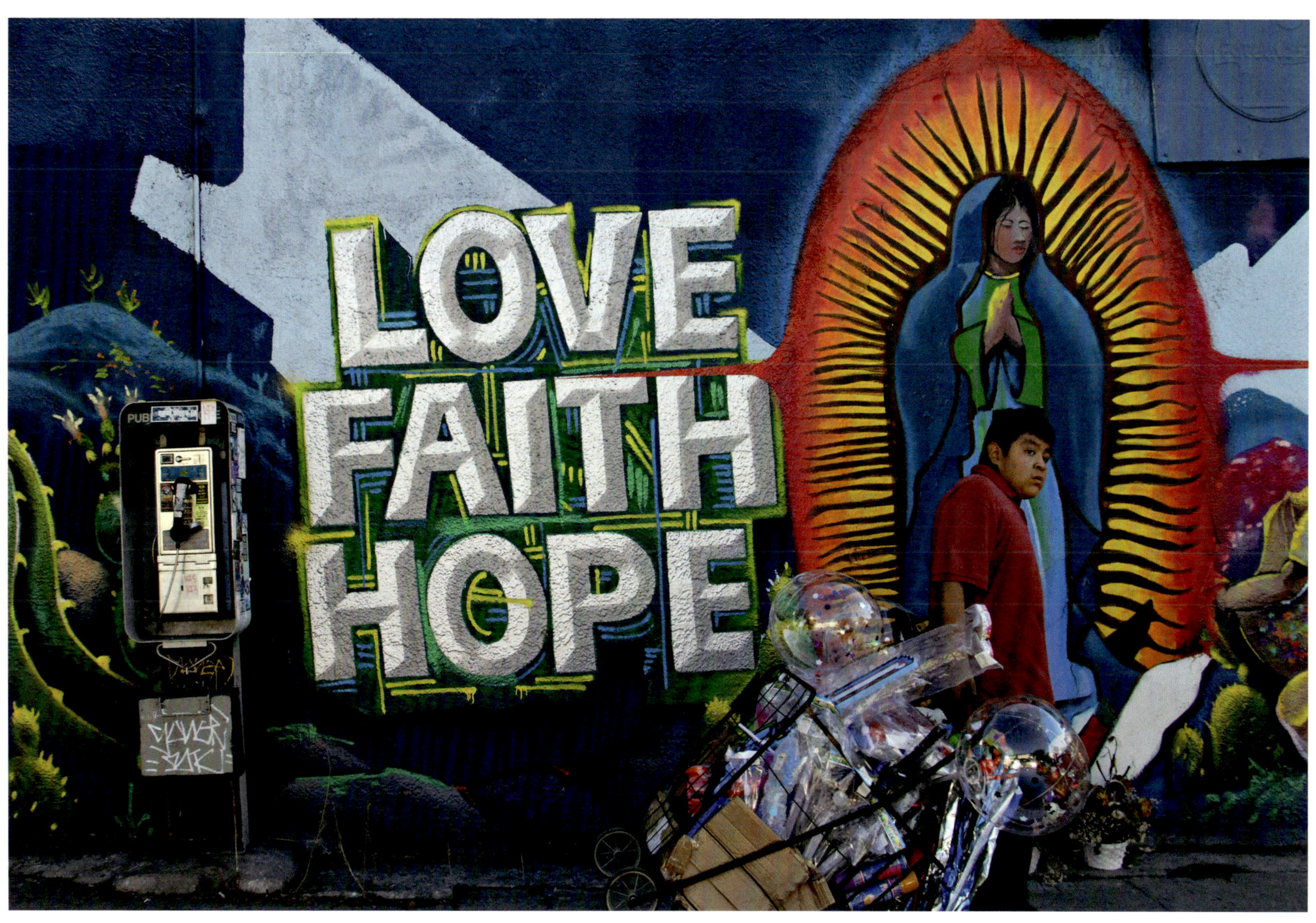
LOVE
FAITH
HOPE

Now, on the streets of Los Angeles, they asked her again for succor from the hard life they faced in a new land. They asked her, too, for refuge from gangs and their graffiti.

Ahora, en las calles de Los Ángeles, ellos volvieron a pedirle socorro de la vida dura que enfrentaban en una tierra nueva. Tambien pidieron a ella un refugio de las pandillas y sus graffitis.

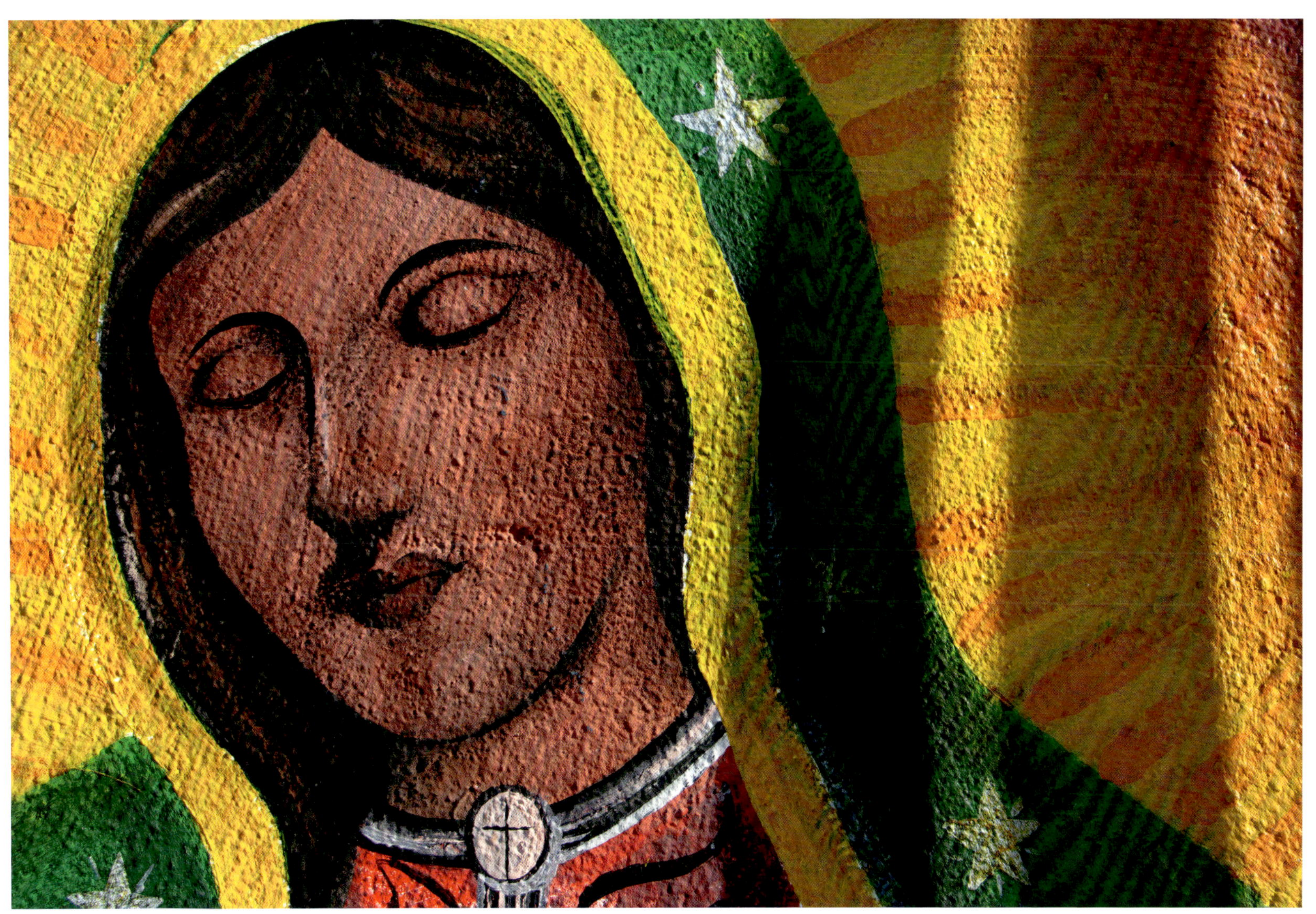

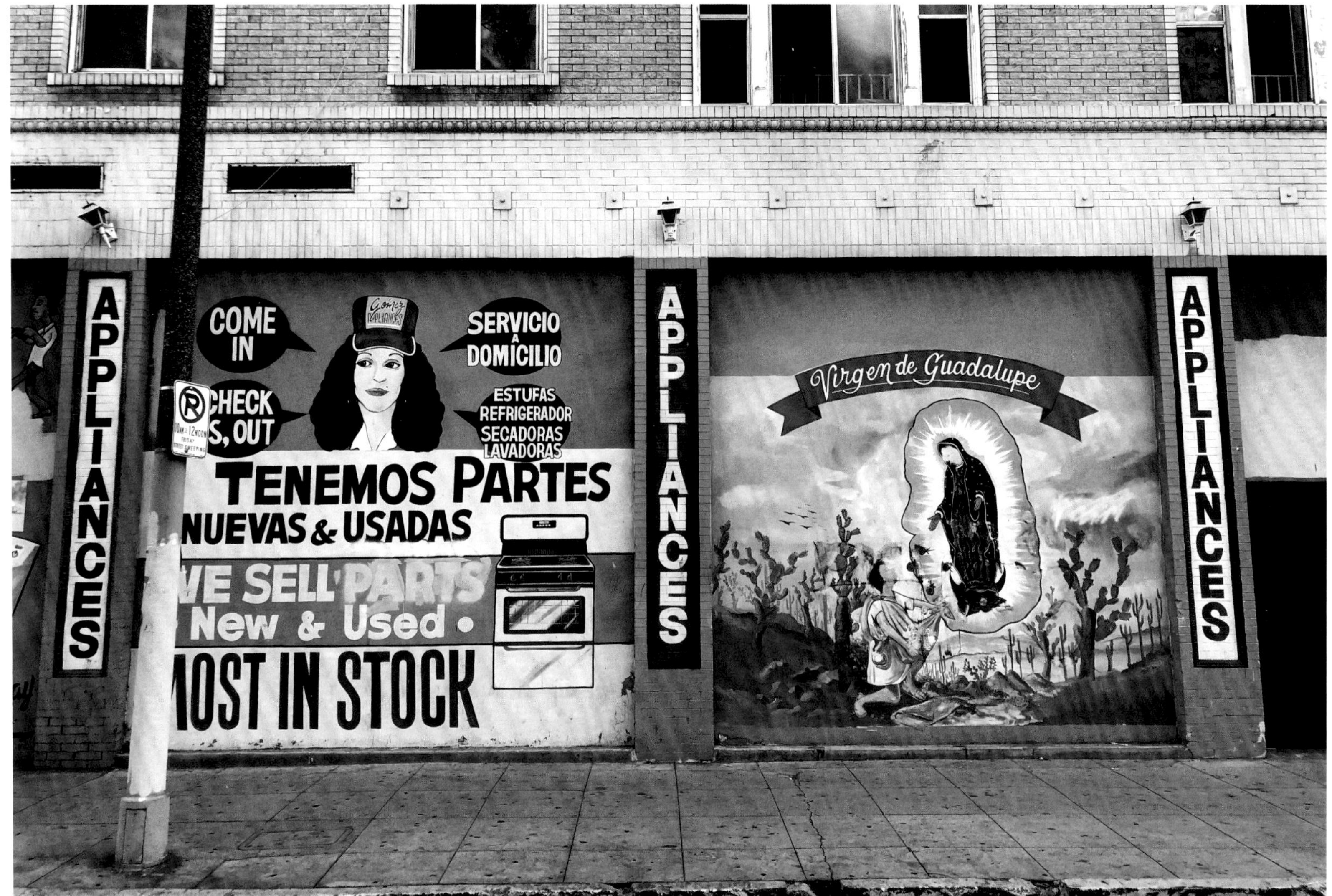
APPLIANCES
COME IN
CHECK S, OUT
SERVICIO A DOMICILIO
ESTUFAS
REFRIGERADOR
SECADORAS
LAVADORAS
TENEMOS PARTES
NUEVAS & USADAS
WE SELL PARTS
New & Used
MOST IN STOCK
APPLIANCES
Virgen de Guadalupe
APPLIANCES

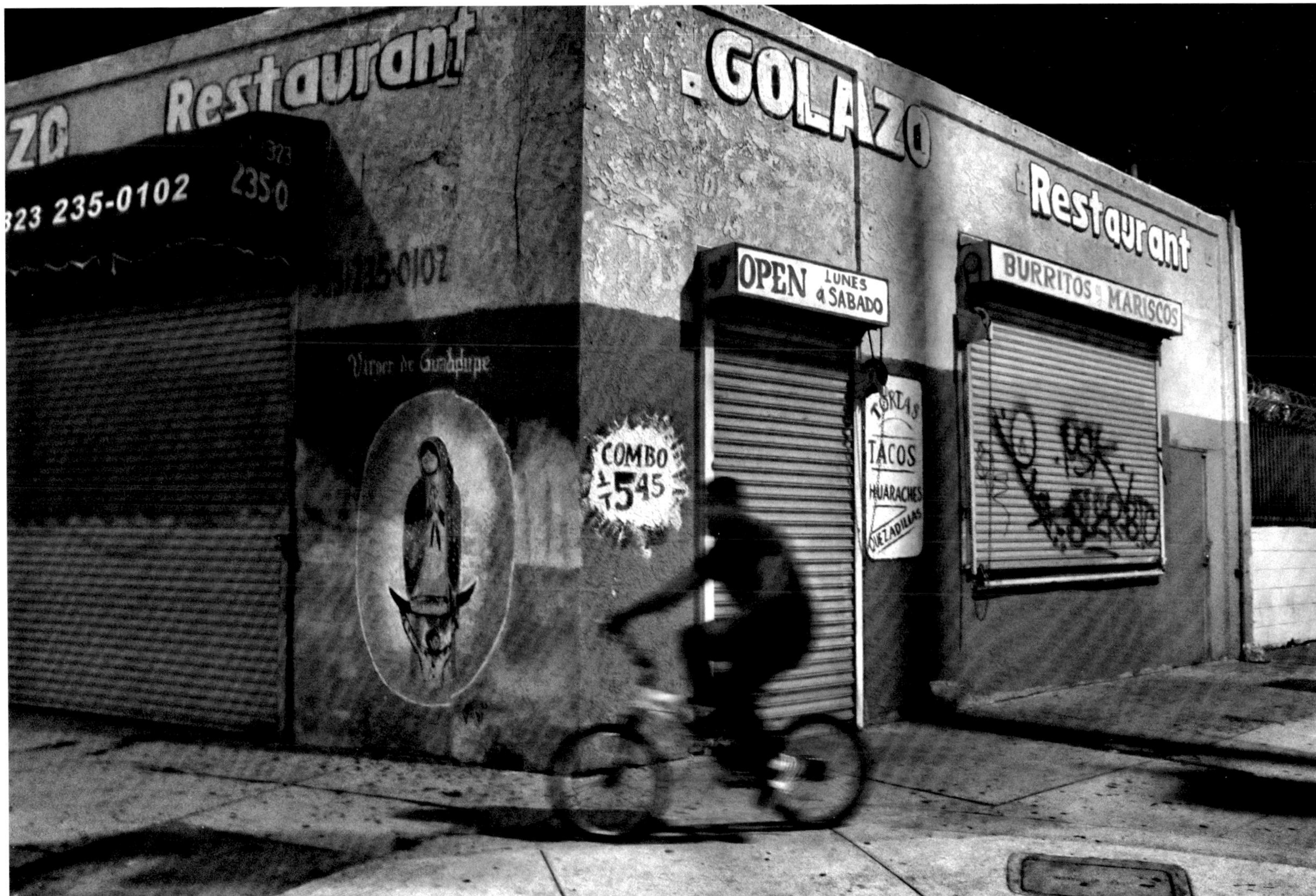

Restaurant
323 235-0102
GOLAZO
Restaurant
OPEN LUNES A SABADO
BURRITOS MARISCOS
Virgen de Guadalupe
COMBO 5.45
TORTAS
TACOS
HUARACHES
QUEZADILLAS

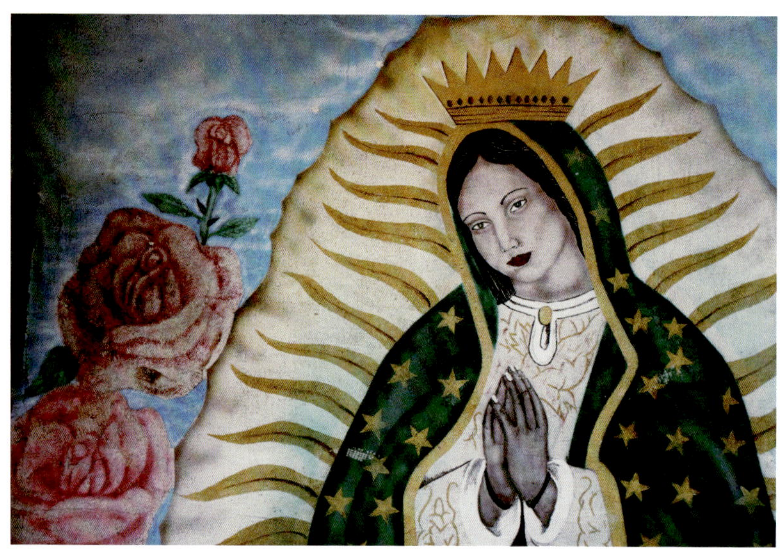

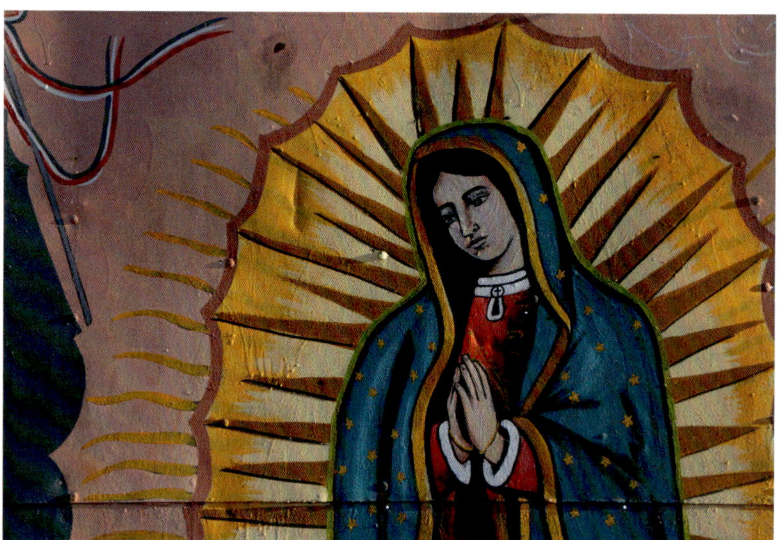

For gang members especially revered her. They etched her on their chests and backs and implored her protection, and would not deface a wall where she appeared.

Los pandilleros le tenían una fuerte reverencia. Ellos se tatuaban en sus pechos y espaldas y le imploraban su protección y no se atrevían a profanar una pared donde ella aparecía.

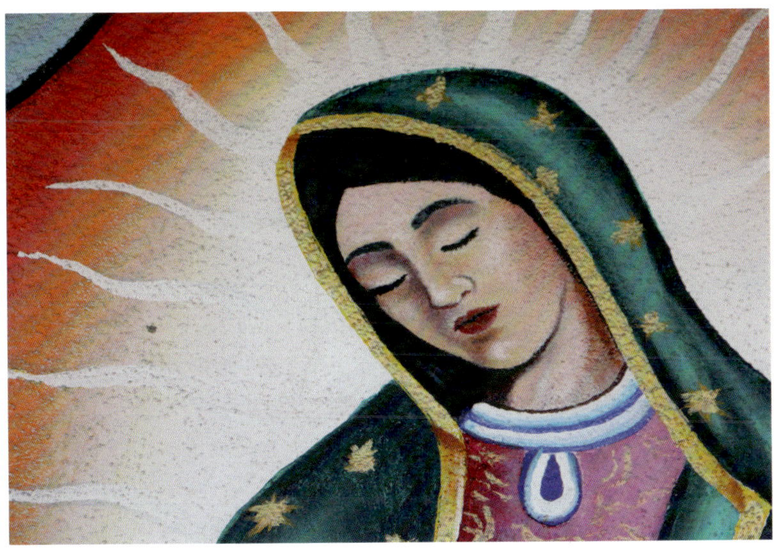

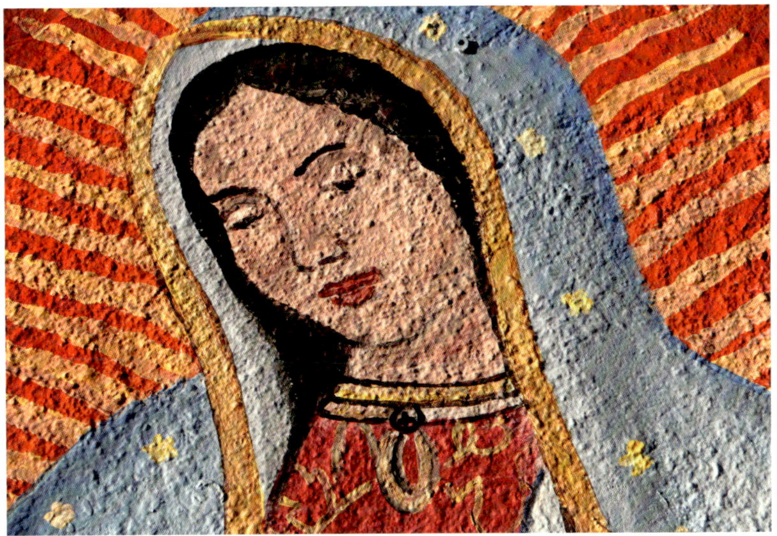

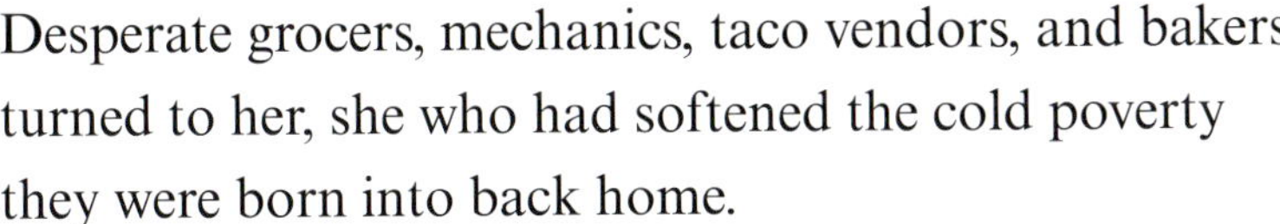

Desperate grocers, mechanics, taco vendors, and bakers turned to her, she who had softened the cold poverty they were born into back home.

Comerciantes, mecánicos, taqueros y panaderos desesperados le recurrieron a ella quien había mitigado la pobreza fría en la que ellos habían nacido en sus pueblos en México.

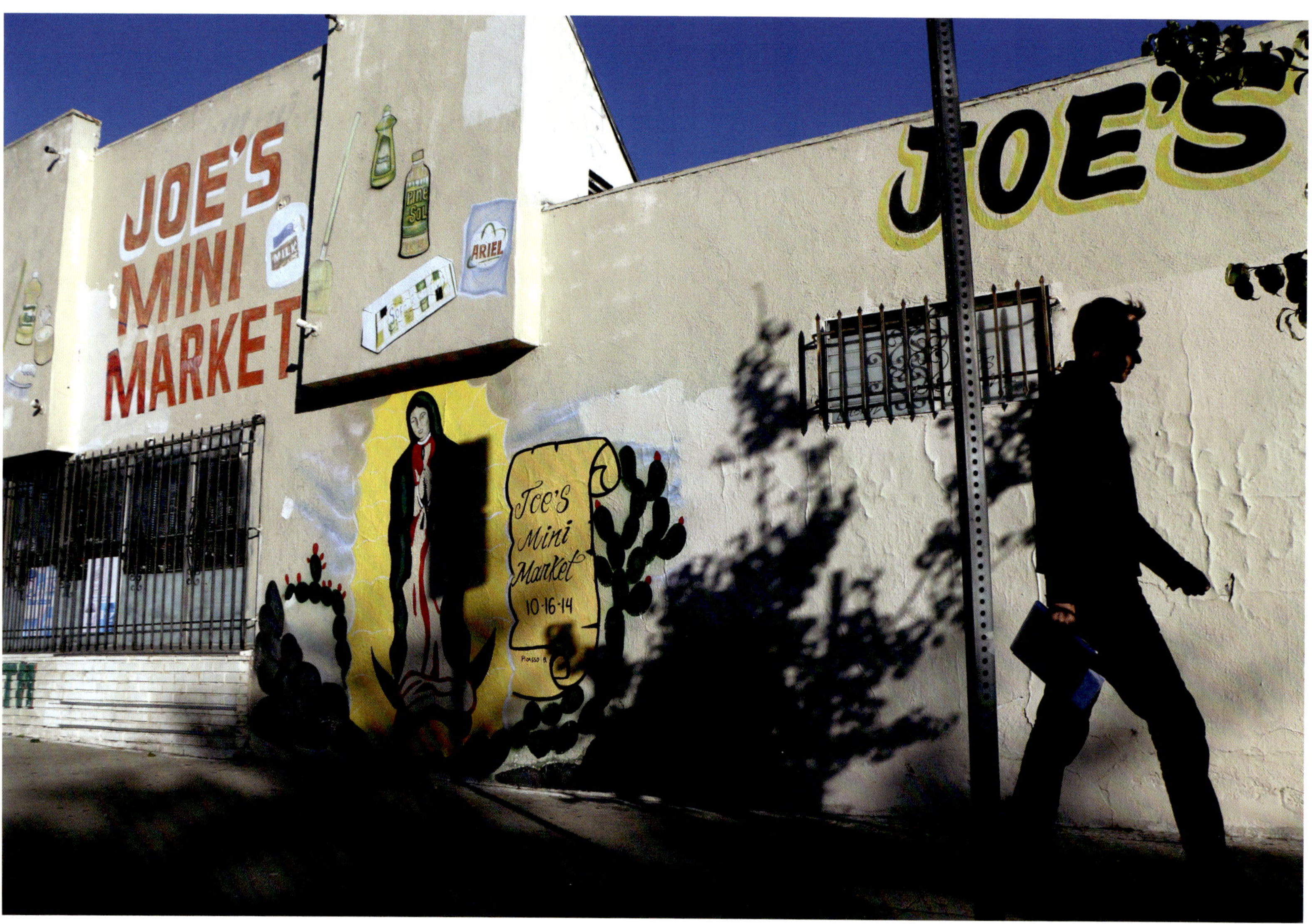
JOE'S
MINI
MARKET
MILK
Pine Sol
ARIEL
Joe's
Mini
Market
10-16-14
JOE'S

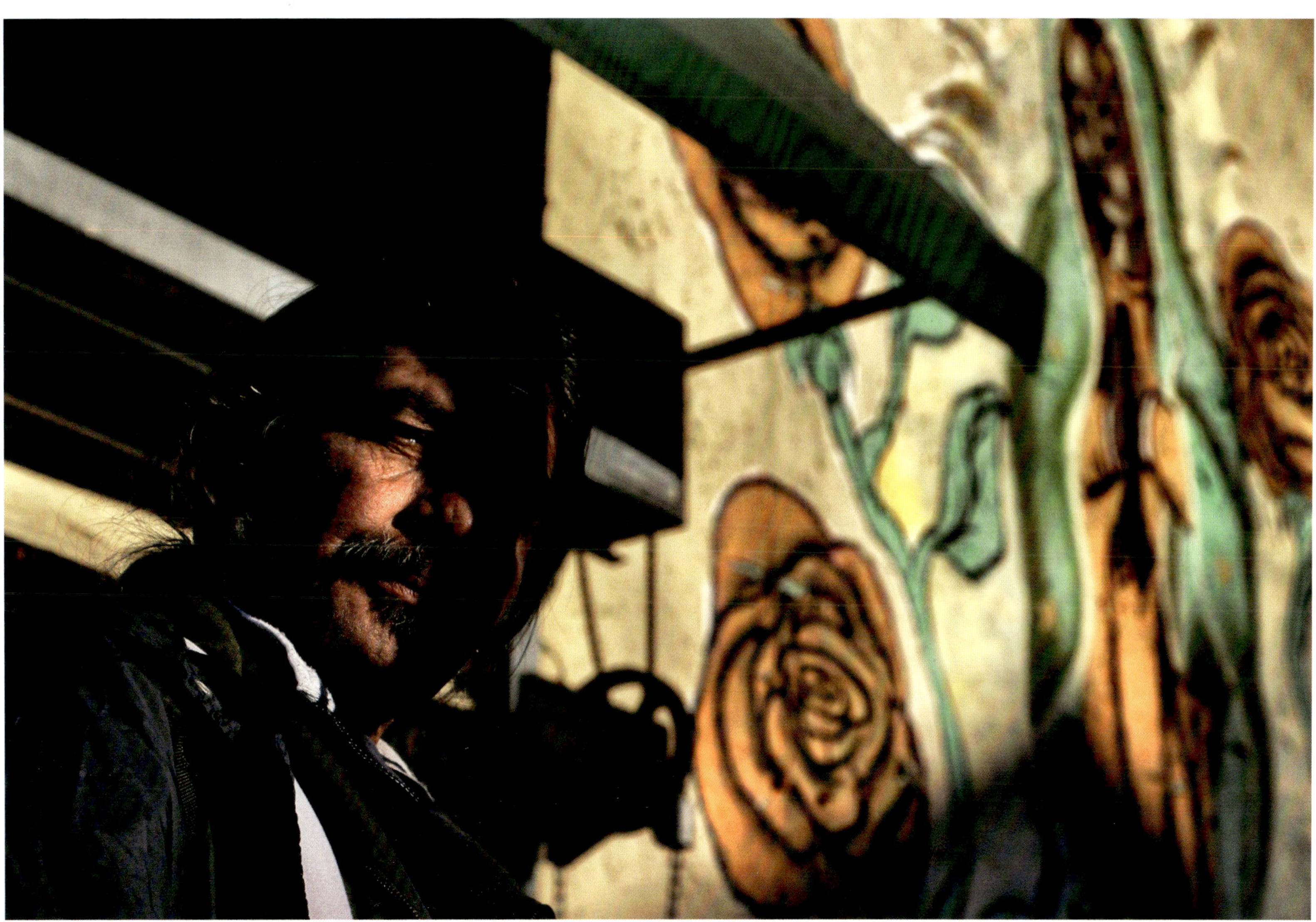

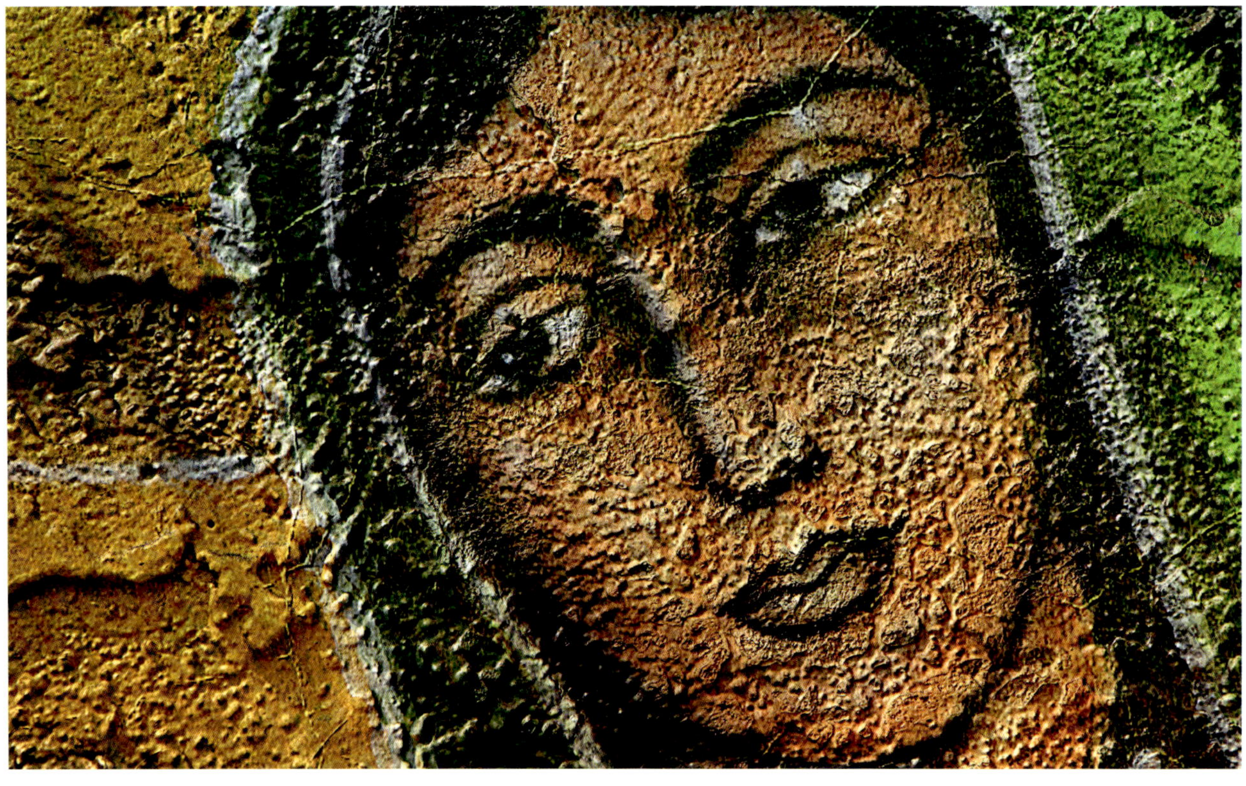

And like a protecting angel, Mexico's Dark Virgin appeared again, this time on the walls of Los Angeles, to people struggling with another new world.

Como un ángel protector, la Virgen Morena de México volvió a aparecer, esta vez en las paredes de Los Ángeles, ante un pueblo que luchaba contra la realidad de otro Nuevo Mundo.

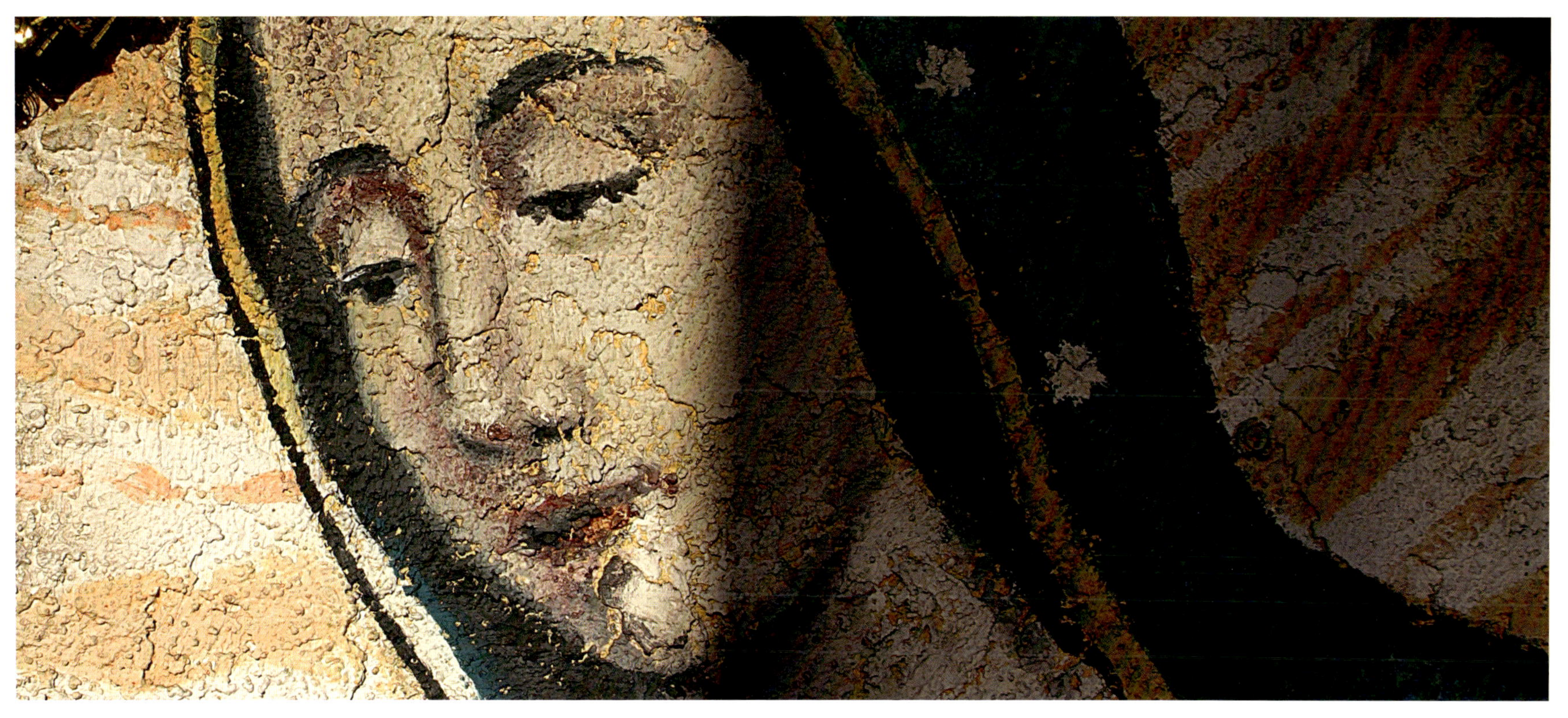

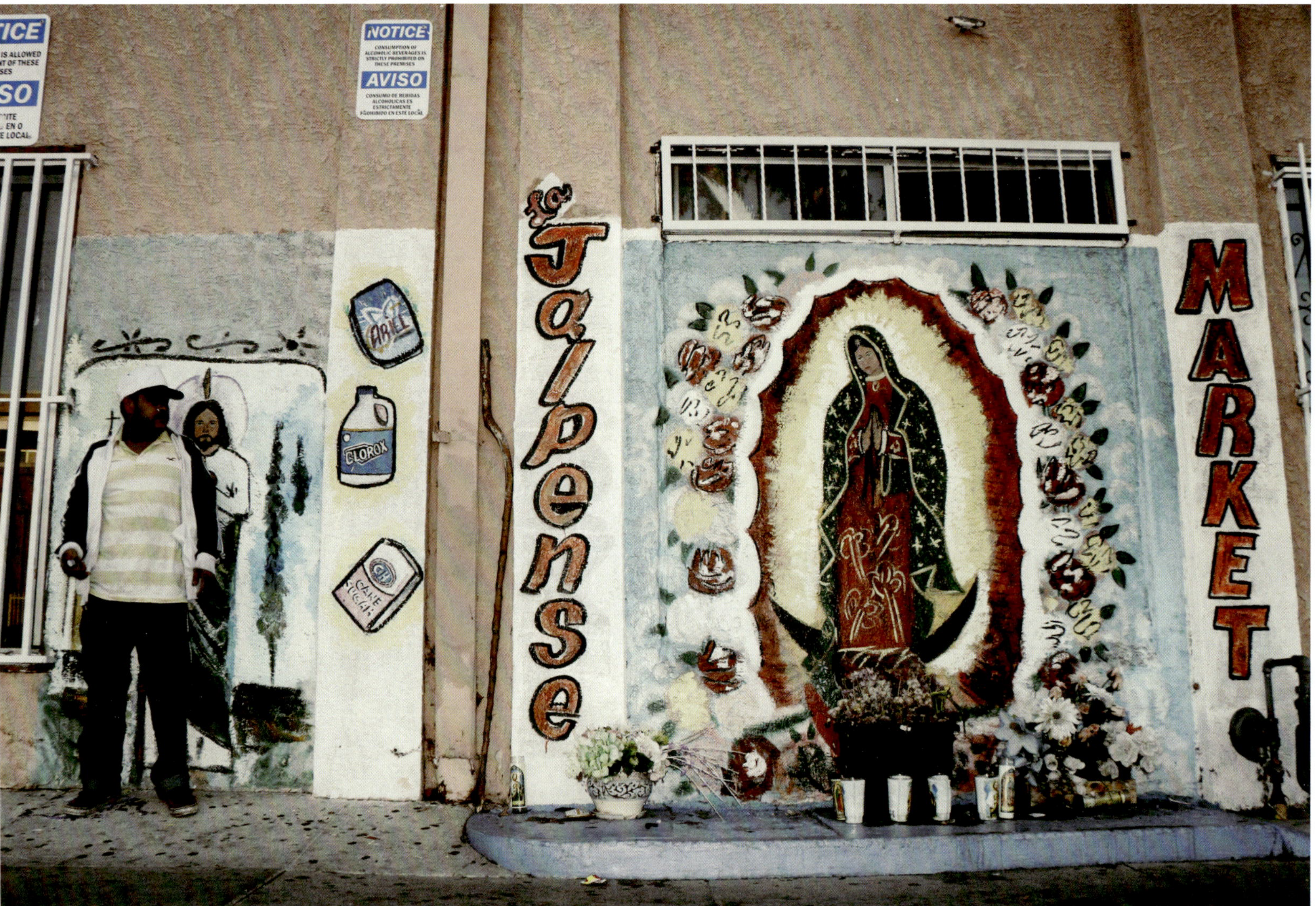
NOTICE
AVISO
CLOROX
la Jalpense
MARKET

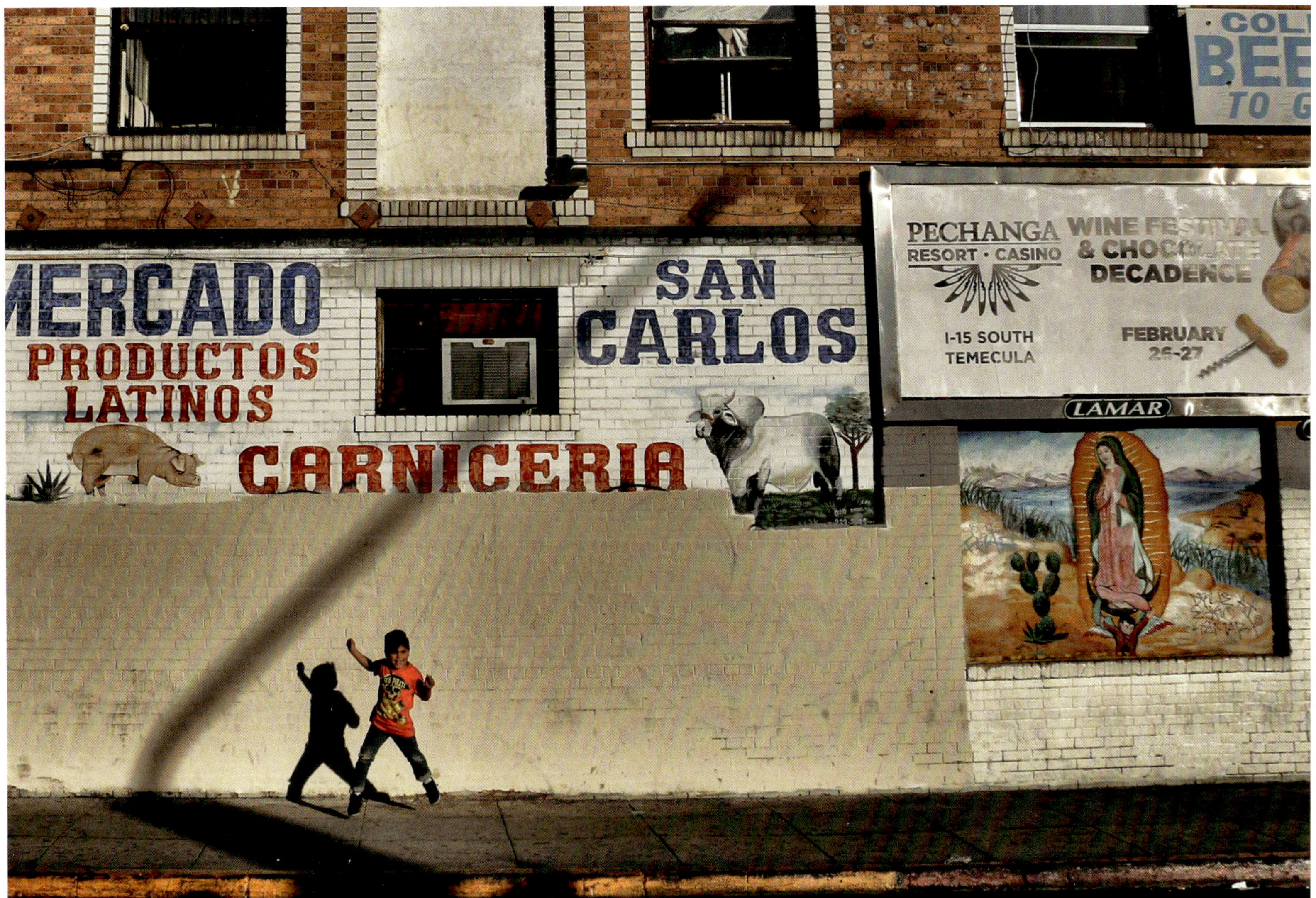

MERCADO
PRODUCTOS
LATINOS
SAN
CARLOS
CARNICERIA
PECHANGA
RESORT · CASINO
DECADENCE
I-15 SOUTH
TEMECULA
FEBRUARY
26-27
LAMAR

She turned those scarred walls into sanctuaries from the blight.

Ella transformó esas paredes manchadas en santuarios contra la desintegración urbana.

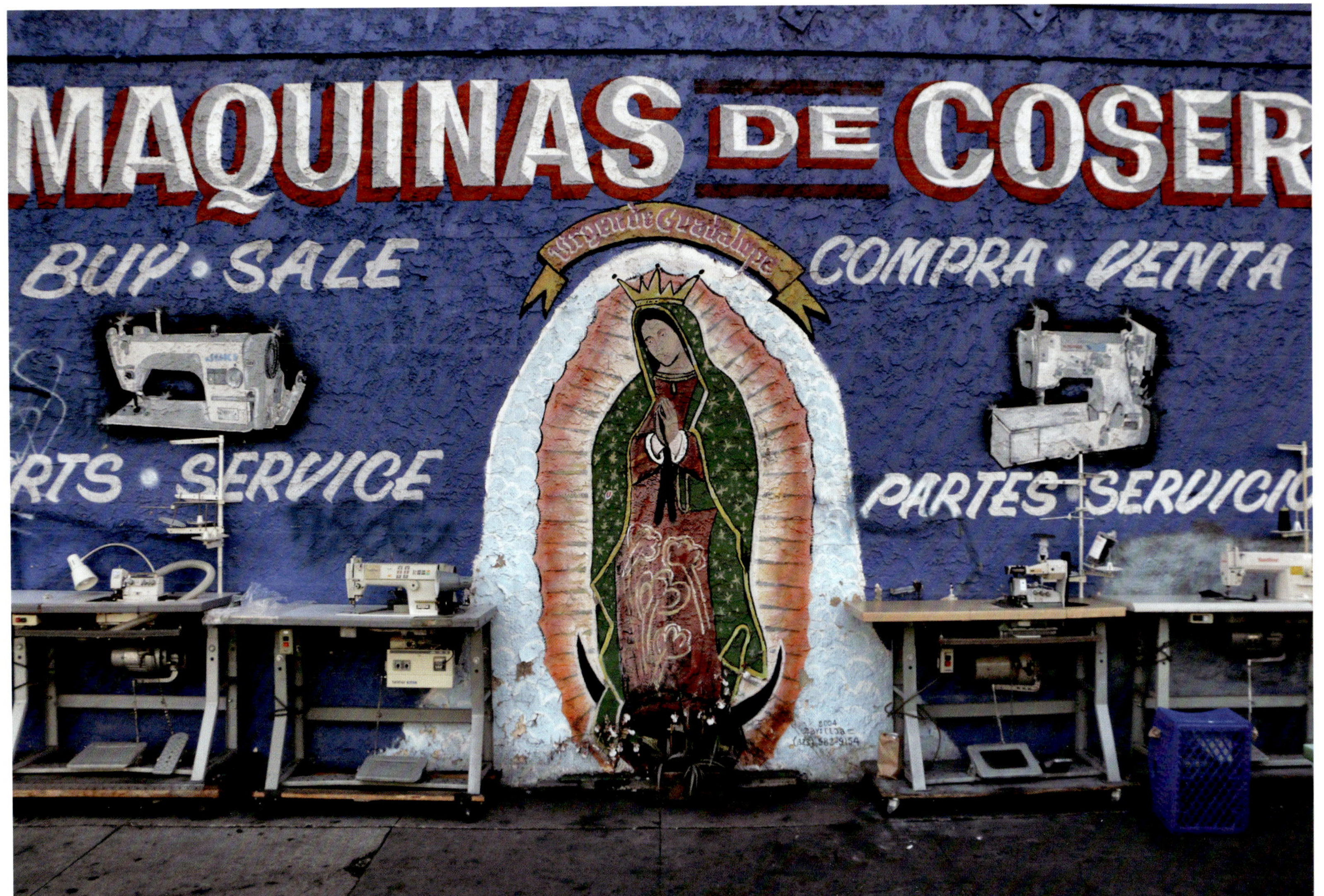
MAQUINAS DE COSER
BUY • SALE
Virgen de Guadalupe
COMPRA • VENTA
RTS • SERVICE
PARTES SERVICI

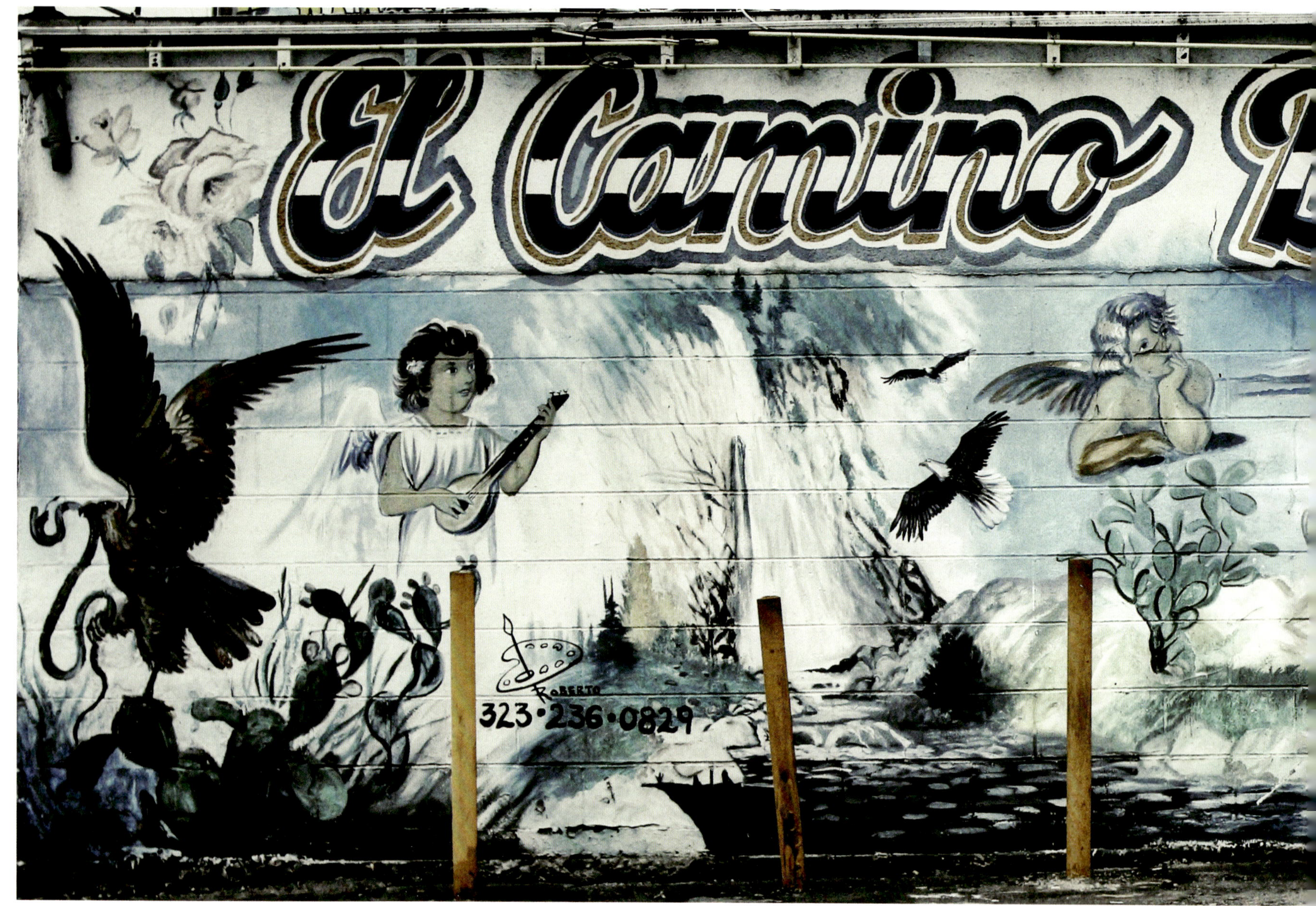
El Camino
ROBERTO
323·236·0829

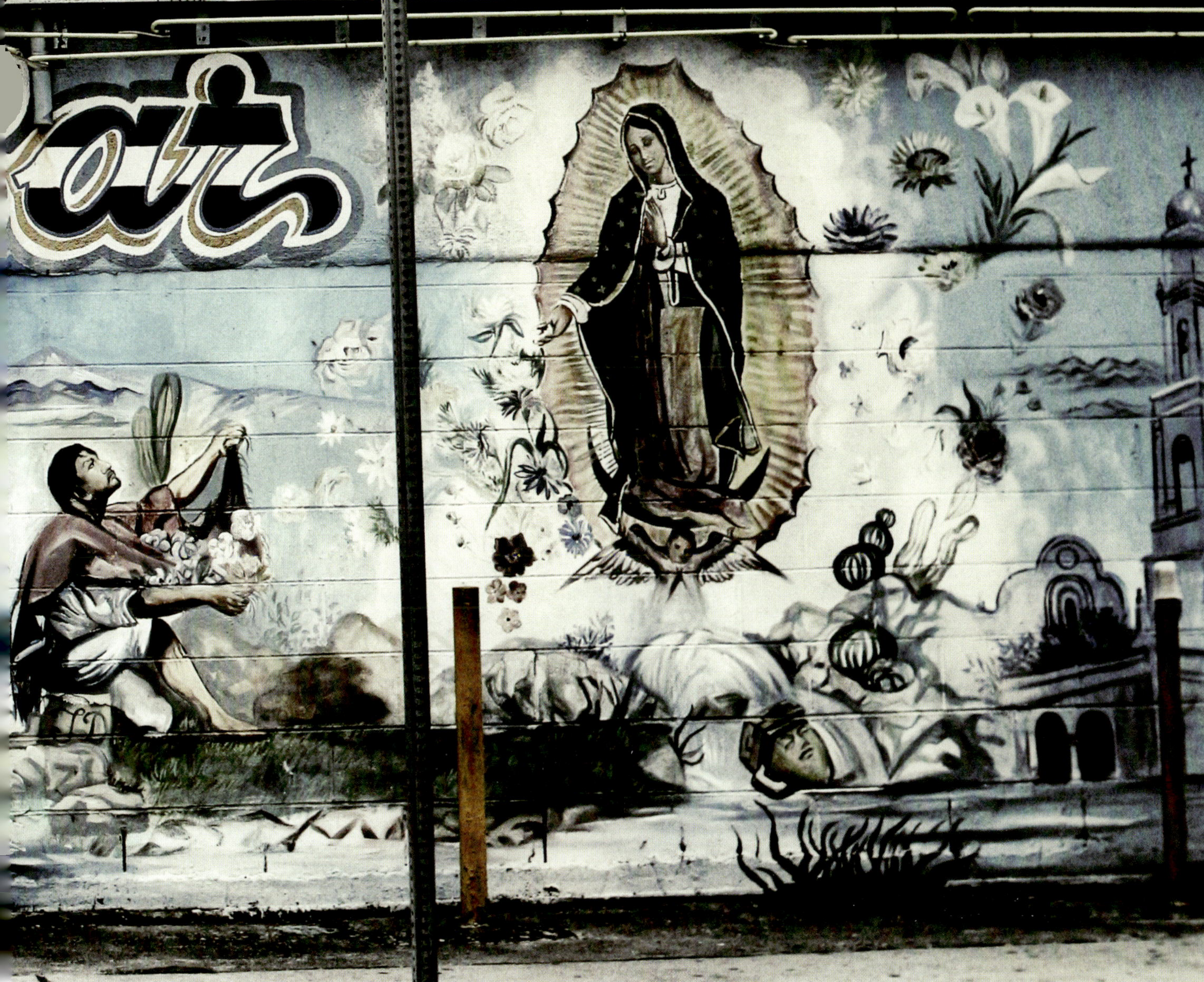

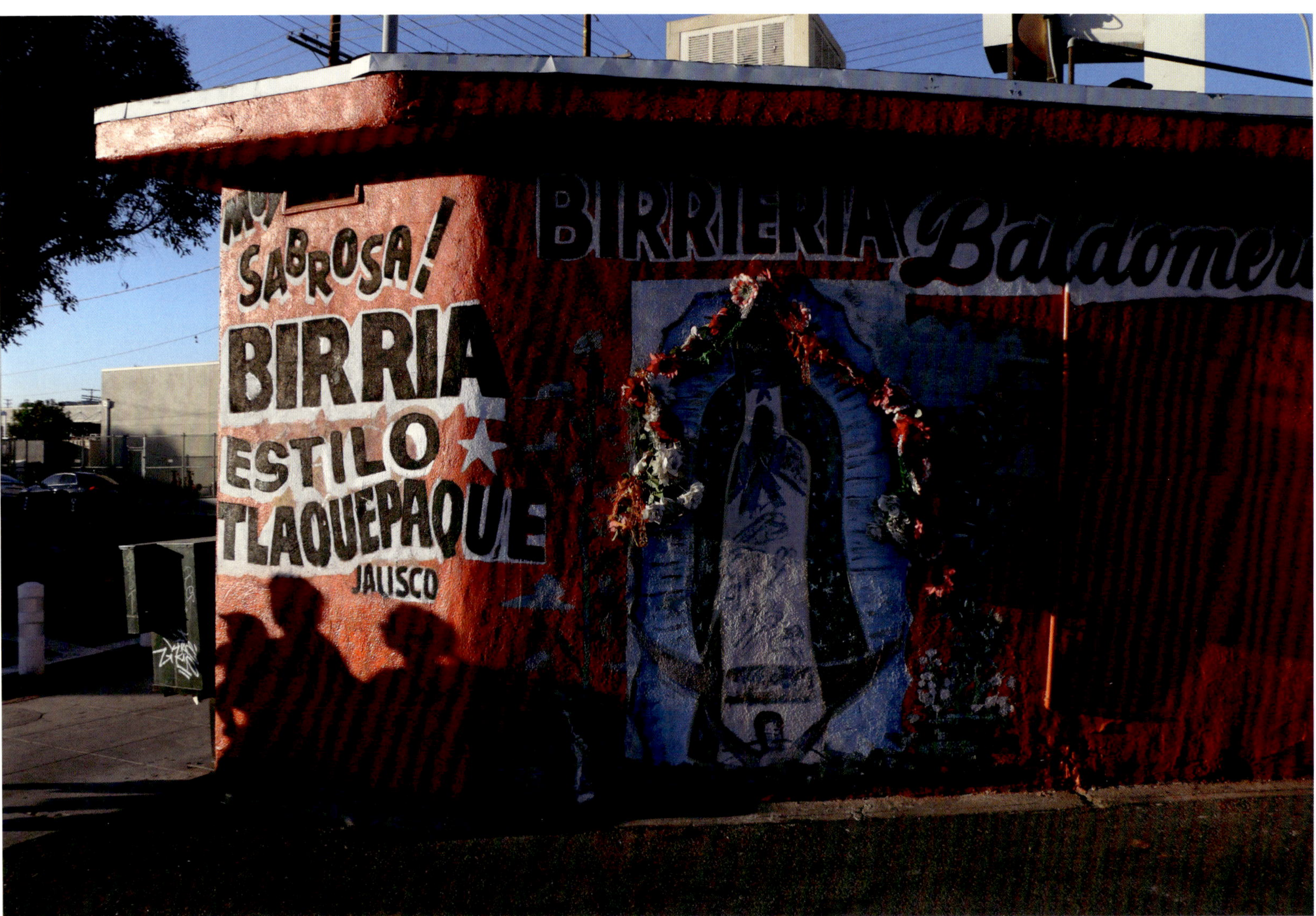
SABROSA!
BIRRIA
ESTILO
TLAQUEPAQUE
JALISCO
BIRRIERIA

A Virgin mural on the wall of a *taquería* or furniture store meant that gangs often spared it the graffiti that they sprayed elsewhere.

Un mural de la Virgen en una pared de una taquería o mueblería provocaba que las pandillas le demostraran misericordia al dueño del negocio en cuanto al grafiti se refiere.

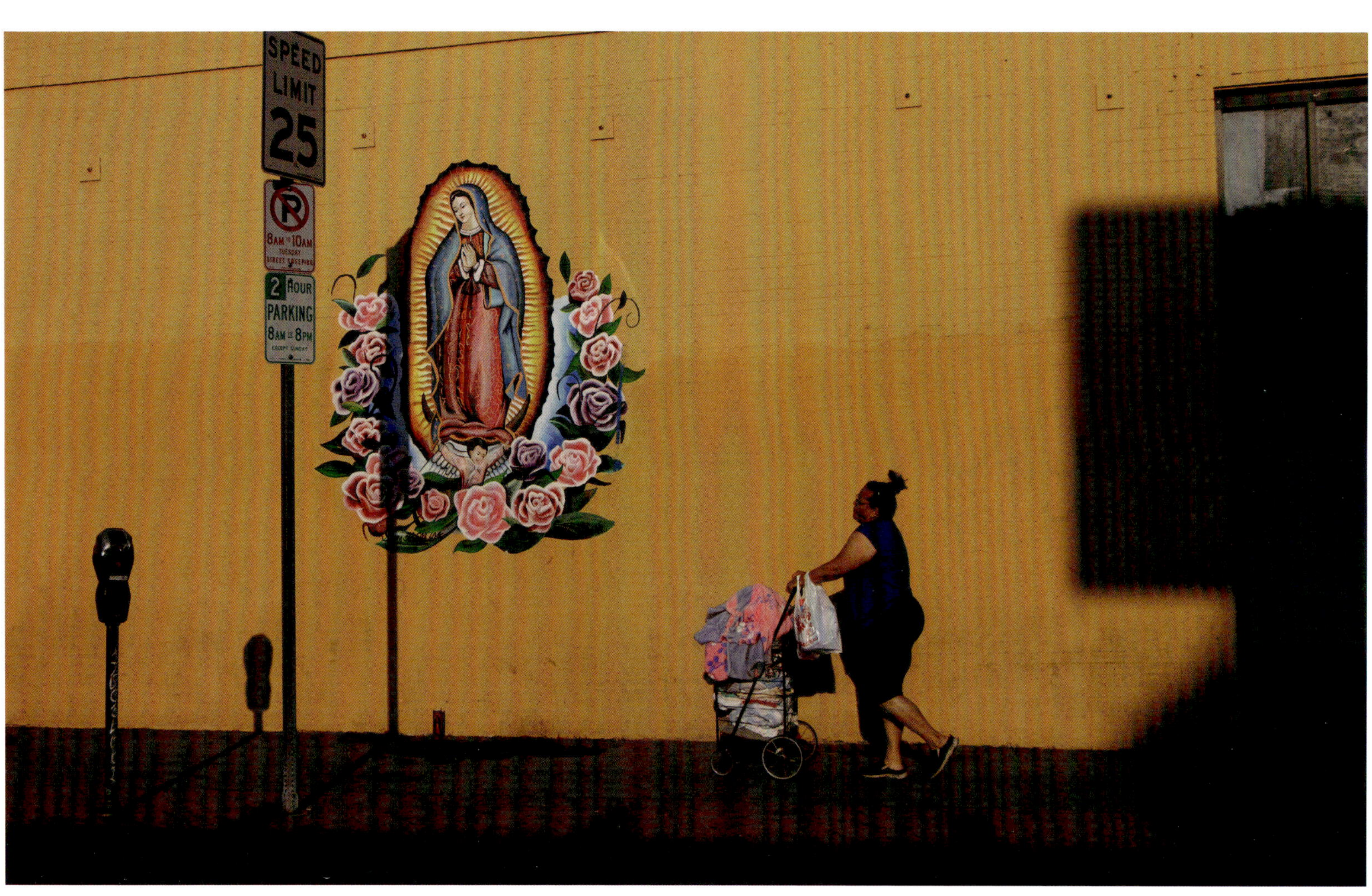
SPEED
LIMIT
25
8AM TO 10AM
2 HOUR
PARKING
8AM TO 8PM

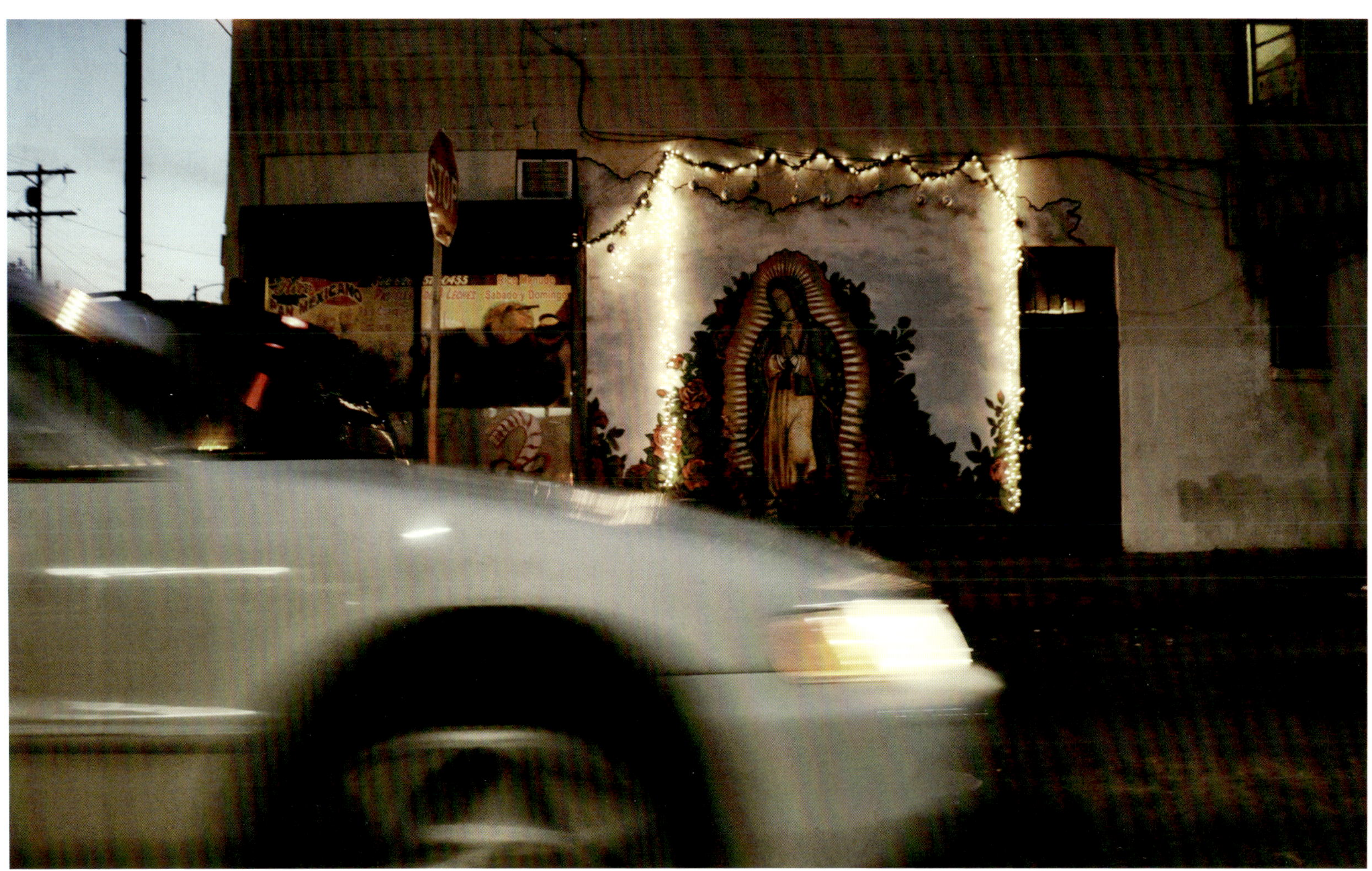
STOP
MEXICANO
Sabado y Domingo

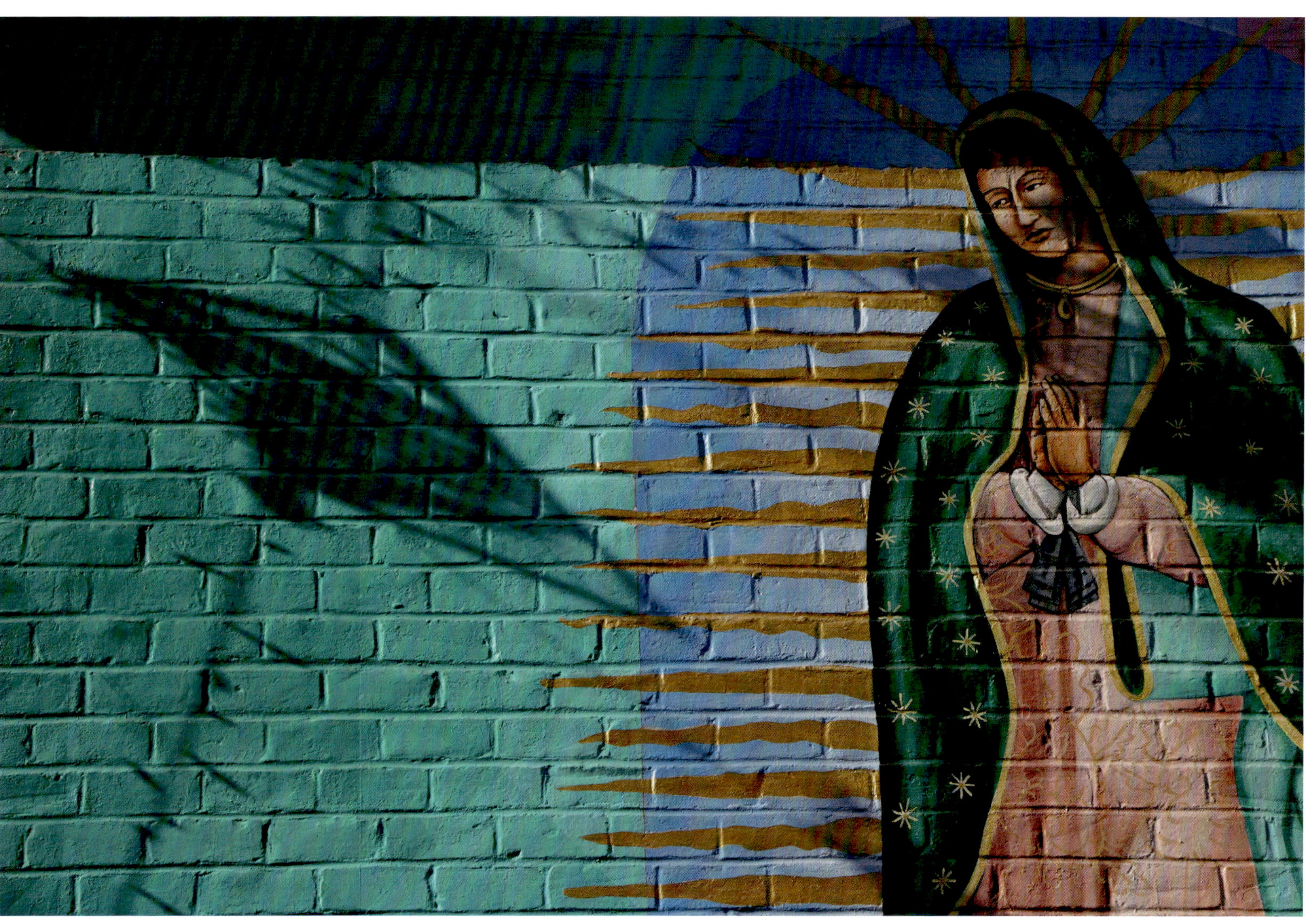

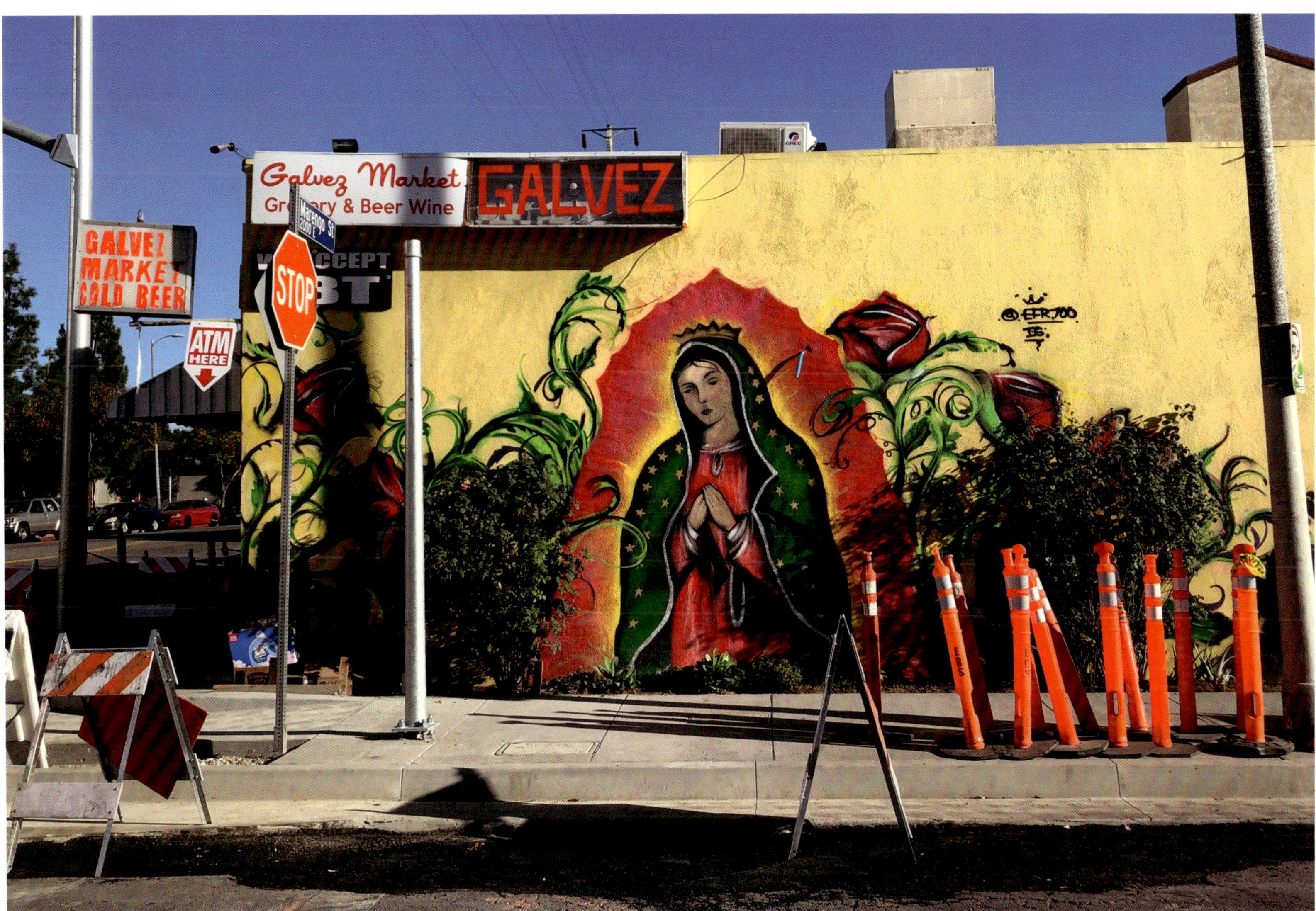
Galvez Market
Grocery & Beer Wine
GALVEZ
GALVEZ
MARKET
COLD BEER
ATM
HERE
STOP
Marengo St
2000 E

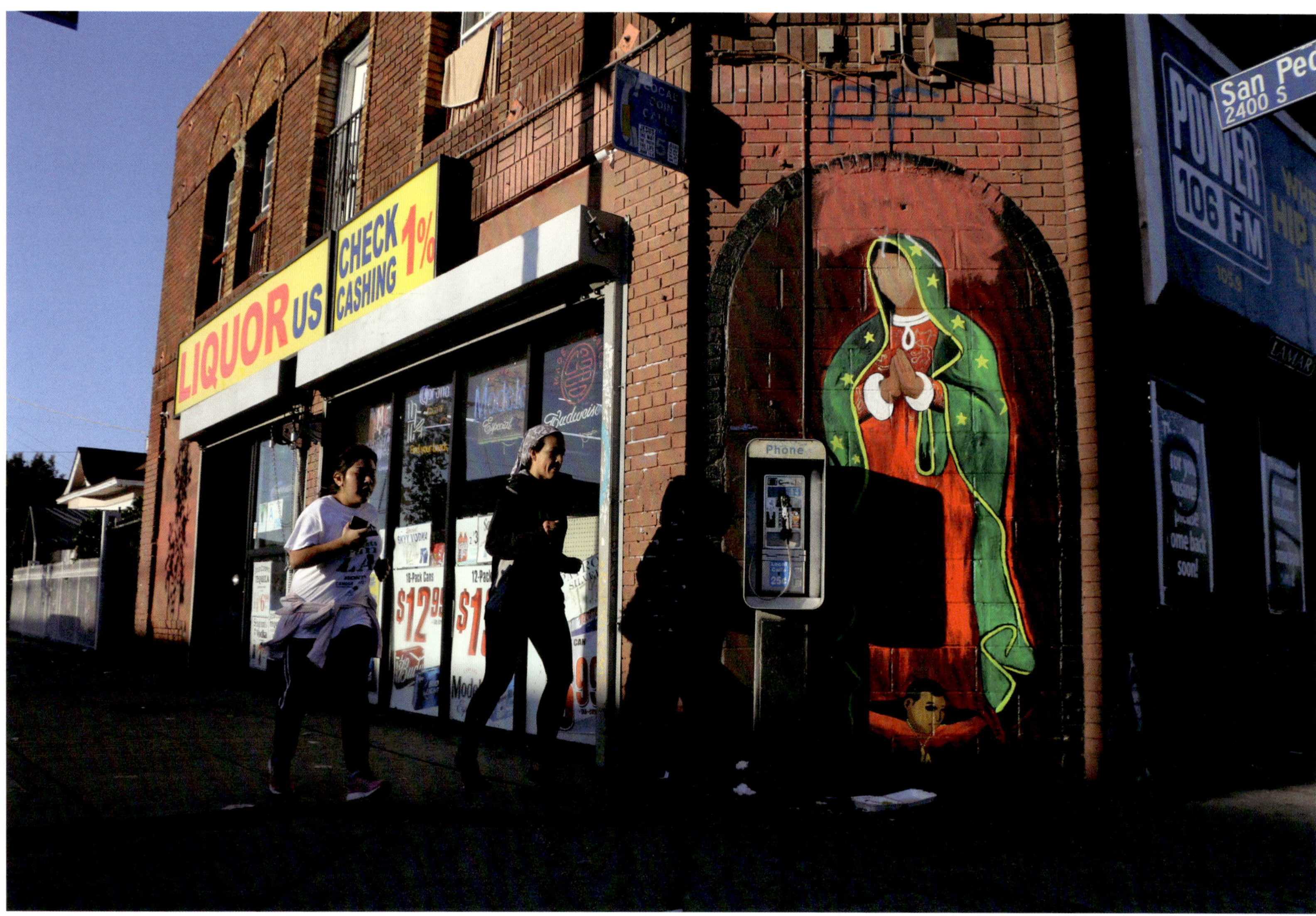
LIQUOR US
CHECK CASHING 1%
LOCAL COIN CALLS
Phone
POWER 106 FM
2400 S
LAMAR
Budweiser
18-Pack Cans
12-Pack

Police presence was intermittent. A mural of the Virgin was about all the private security these immigrant entrepreneurs could afford.

La presencia de policía era escasa. Un mural de la Virgen era toda la seguridad privada que estos empresarios migrantes podían pagar.

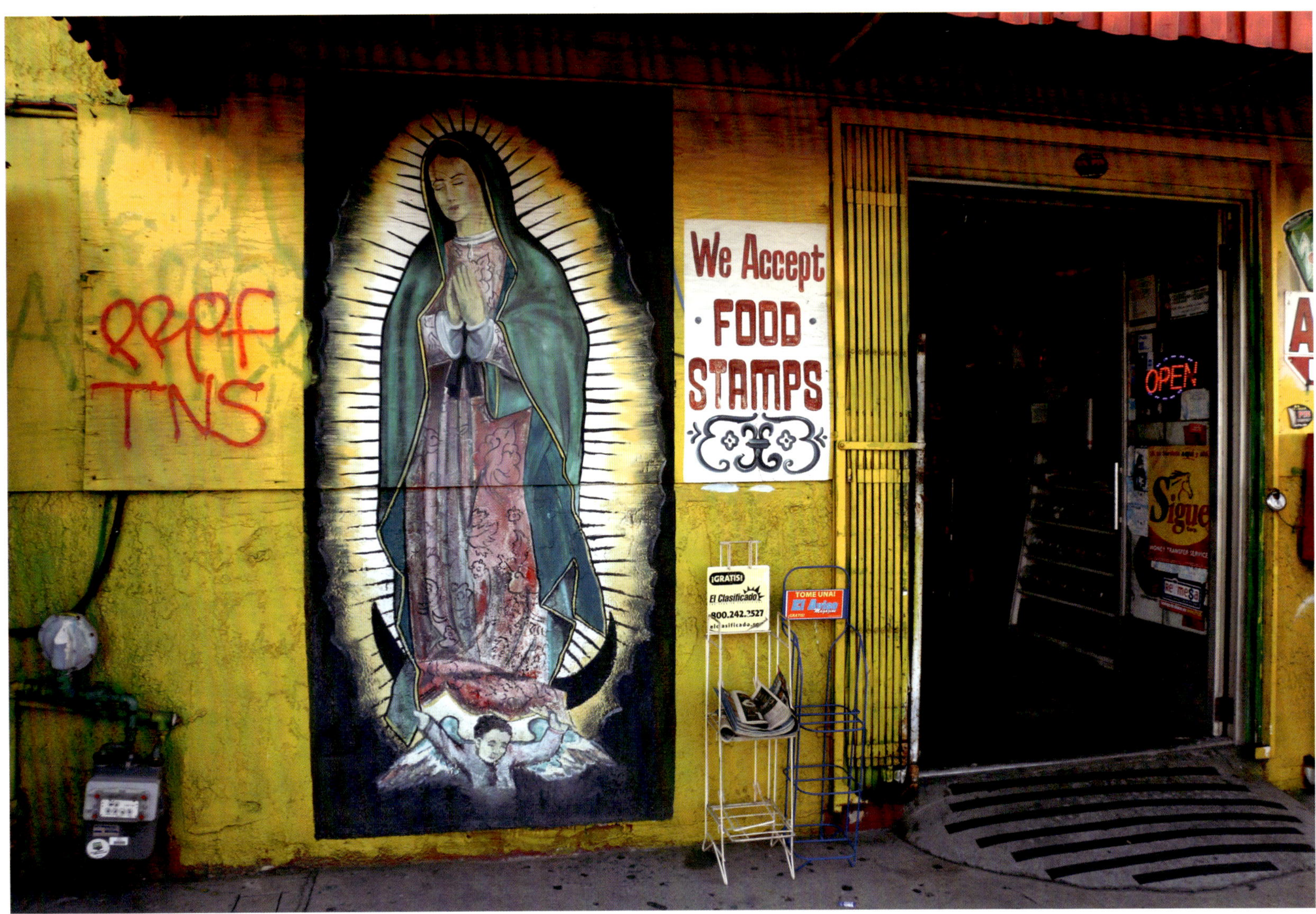
We Accept
FOOD
STAMPS
OPEN
¡GRATIS!
El Clasificado
800.242.2527
TOME UNA!
Sigue

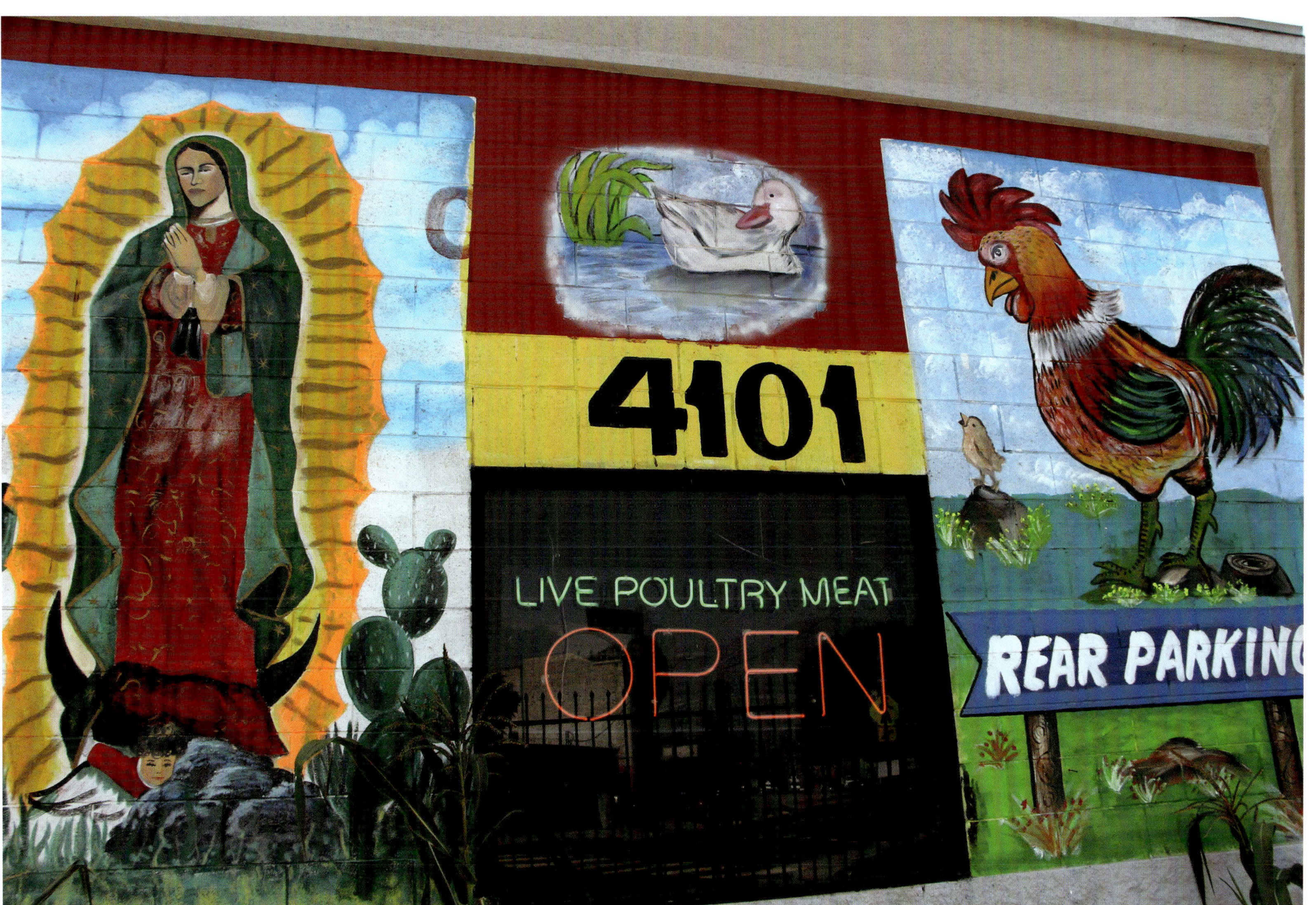
4101
LIVE POULTRY MEAT
OPEN
REAR PARKING

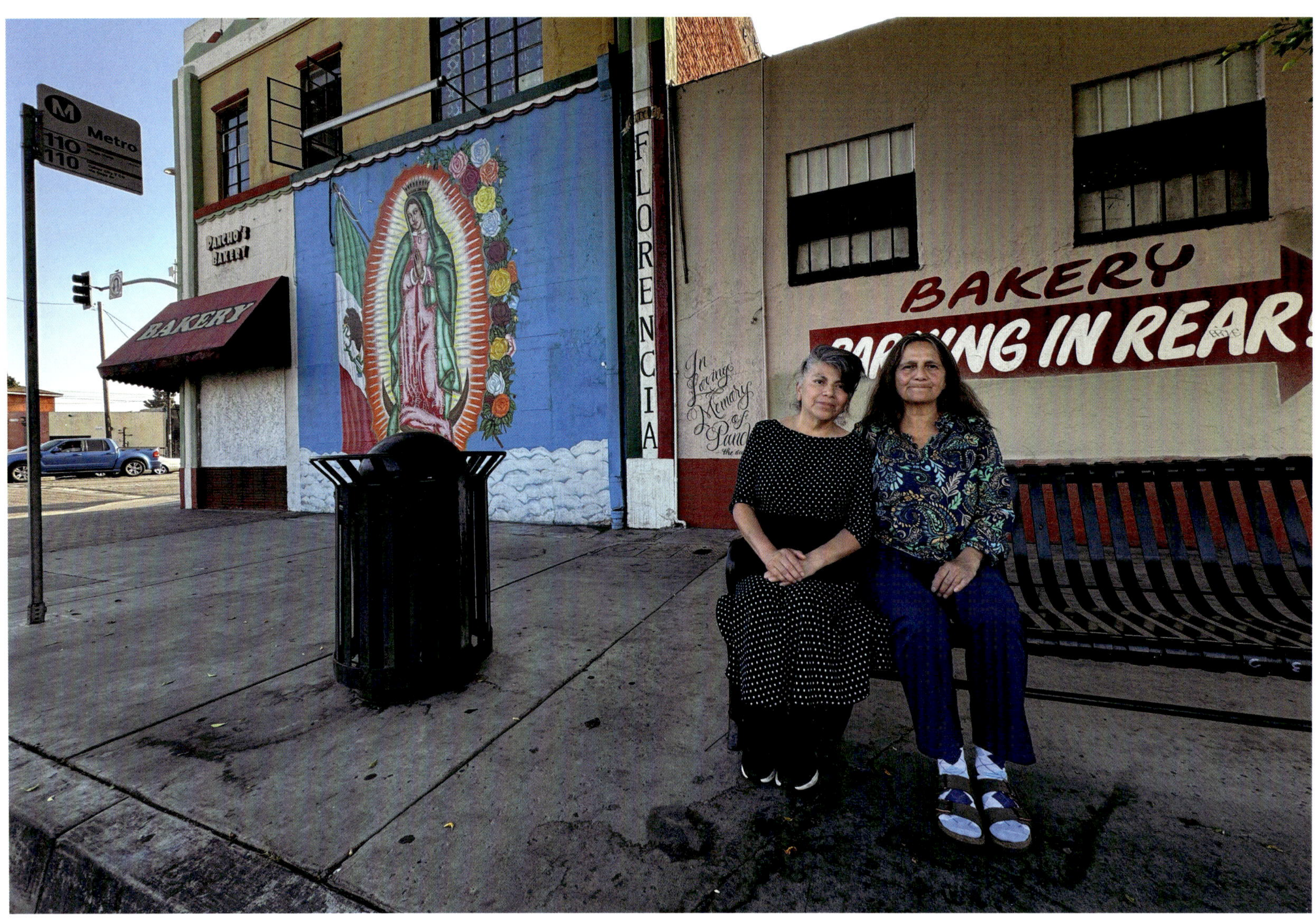

M
Metro
110
110
PANCHO'S BAKERY
BAKERY
FLORENCIA
In Loving Memory of
BAKERY
NG IN REAR!

She was about all the advertising they could afford, as well. In Los Angeles, she appeared alongside bottles of bleach and corn oil, cellphones and milk cartons, letting customers know that she might bless both the store and the person who shopped there.

Ella era también toda la publicidad que estas tiendas podían costear. En Los Ángeles, ella aparecía junto a botellas de blanqueador y aceite de maíz, teléfonos celulares y cartones de leche, dejándoles saber a los clientes que ella quizá podría bendecir tanto a la tienda como a la persona que hacía sus compras allí.

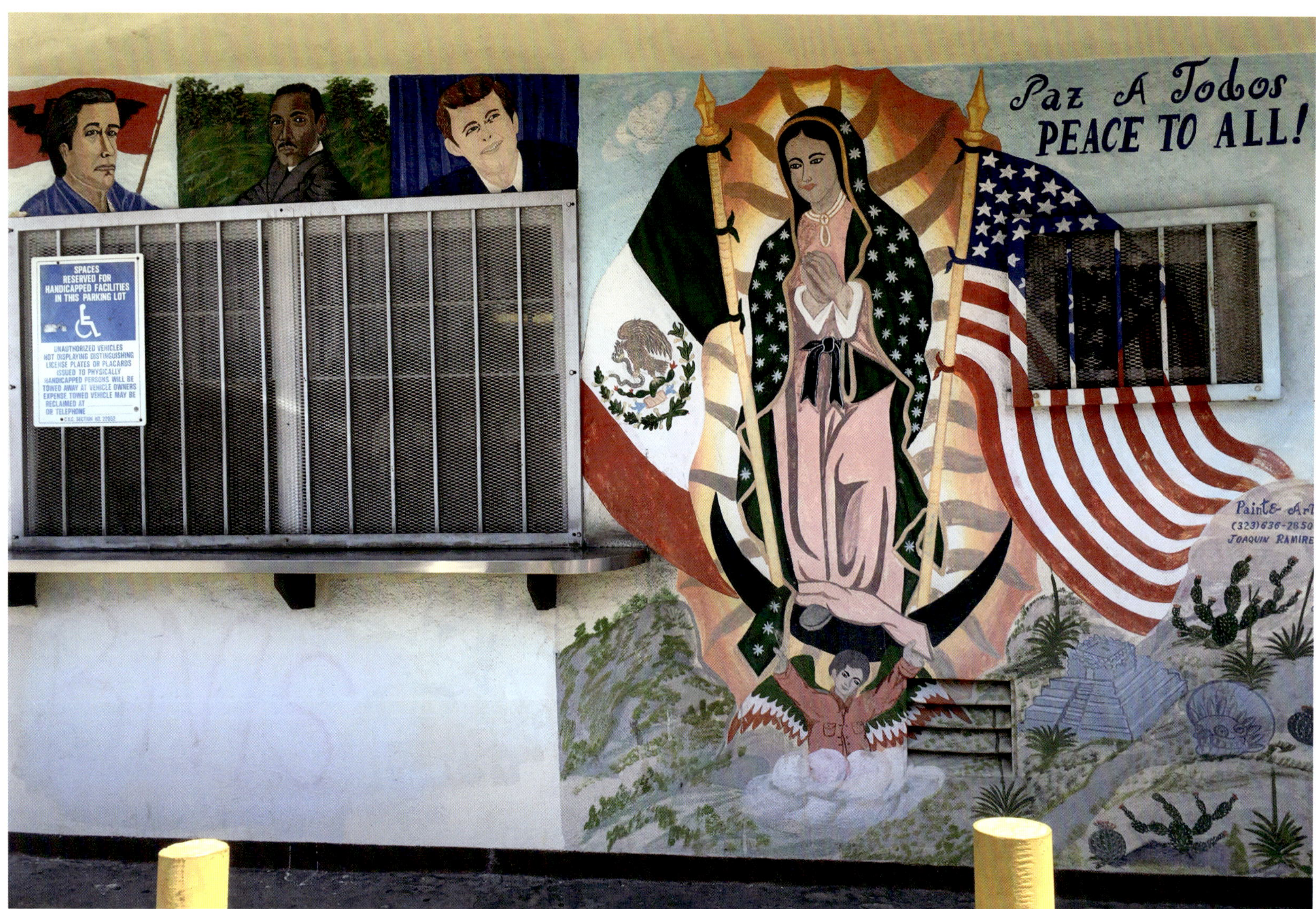
Paz A Todos
PEACE TO ALL!
SPACES
RESERVED FOR
HANDICAPPED FACILITIES
IN THIS PARKING LOT
UNAUTHORIZED VEHICLES
NOT DISPLAYING DISTINGUISHING
LICENSE PLATES OR PLACARDS
ISSUED TO PHYSICALLY
HANDICAPPED PERSONS WILL BE
TOWED AWAY AT VEHICLE OWNERS
EXPENSE. TOWED VEHICLE MAY BE
RECLAIMED AT
OR TELEPHONE
C.V.C. SECTION NO. 22652
Painte-Ar
(323)636-2850
JOAQUIN RAMIRE

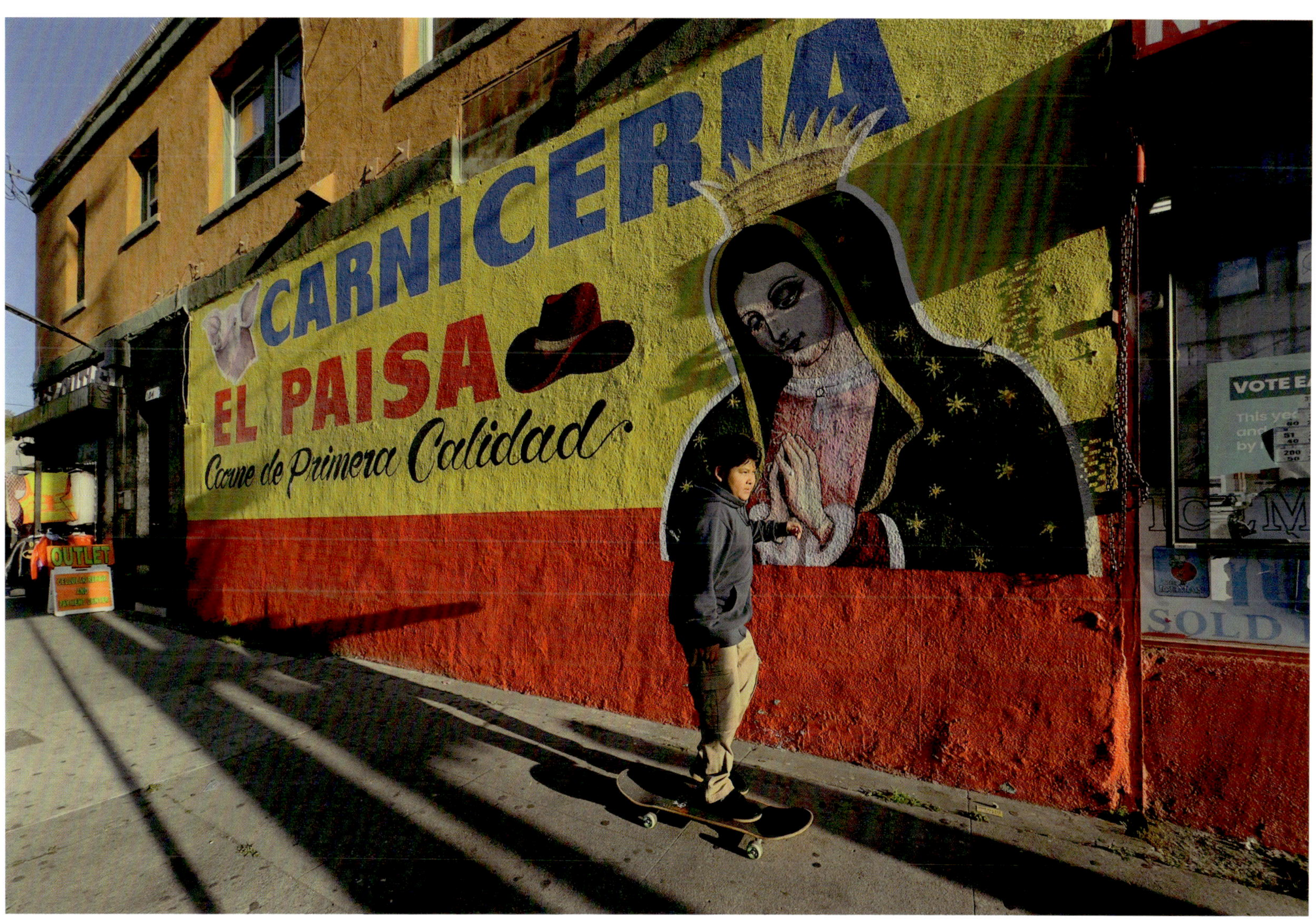
CARNICERIA
EL PAISA
Carne de Primera Calidad
OUTLET

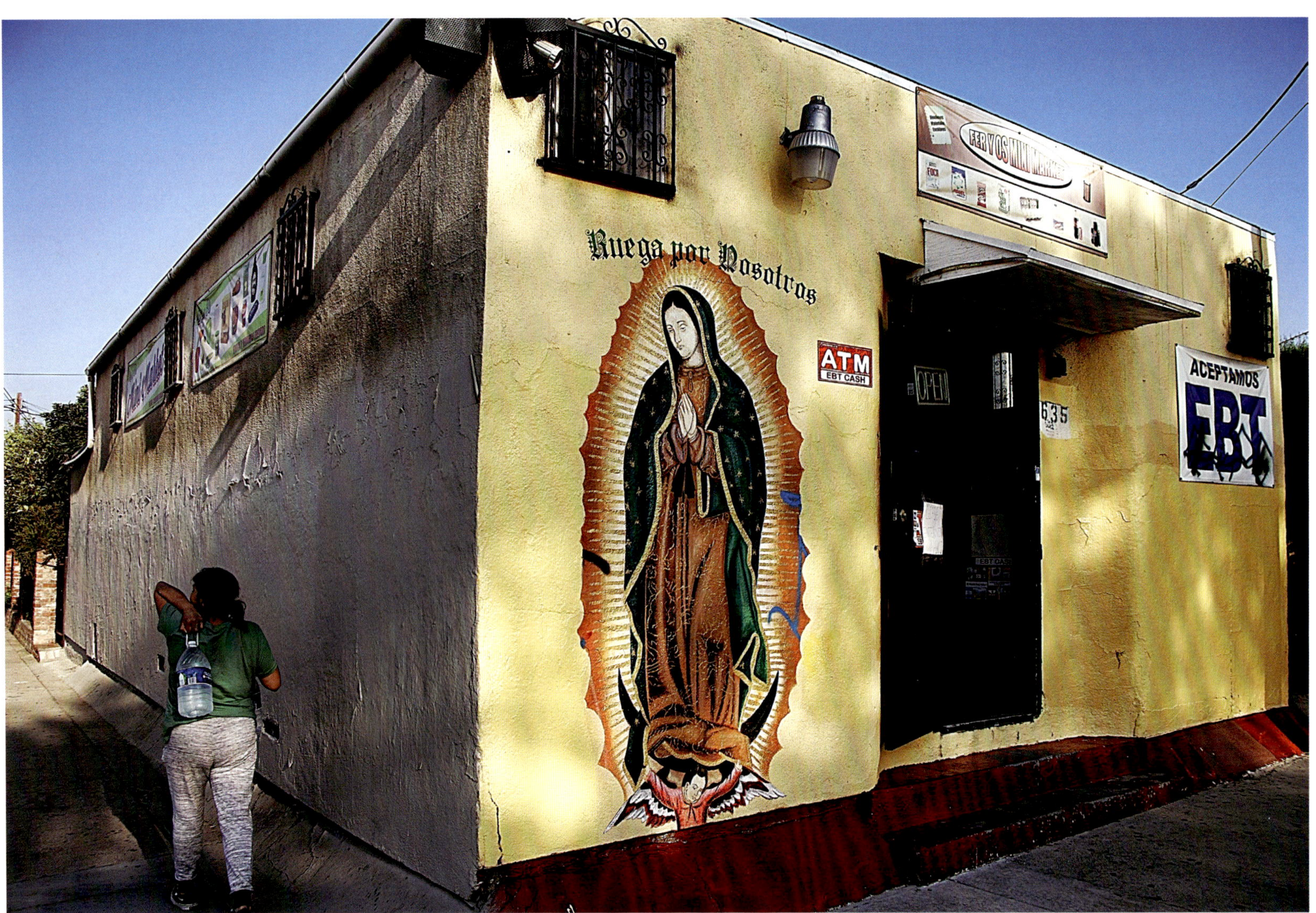
FER Y OS MINI MARKET
Ruega por Nosotros
ATM
EBT CASH
OPEN
635
ACEPTAMOS
EBT

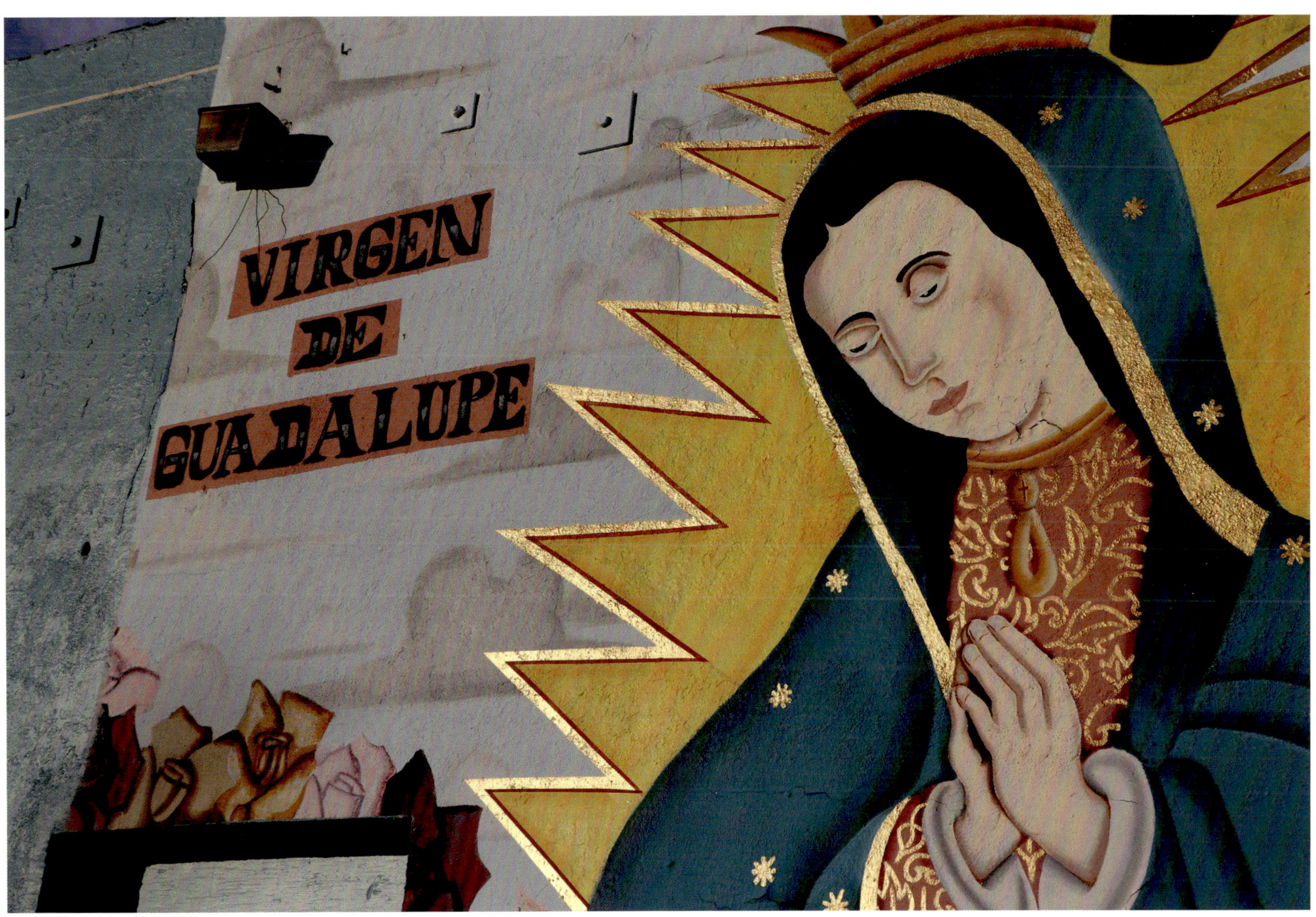
VIRGEN
DE
GUADALUPE

The customers of these shops also needed her protection, for the jobs they found in Los Angeles provided little safety.

Los clientes de esas tiendas también necesitaban protección porque los empleos que ellos encontraban en Los Ángeles les daban poca seguridad.

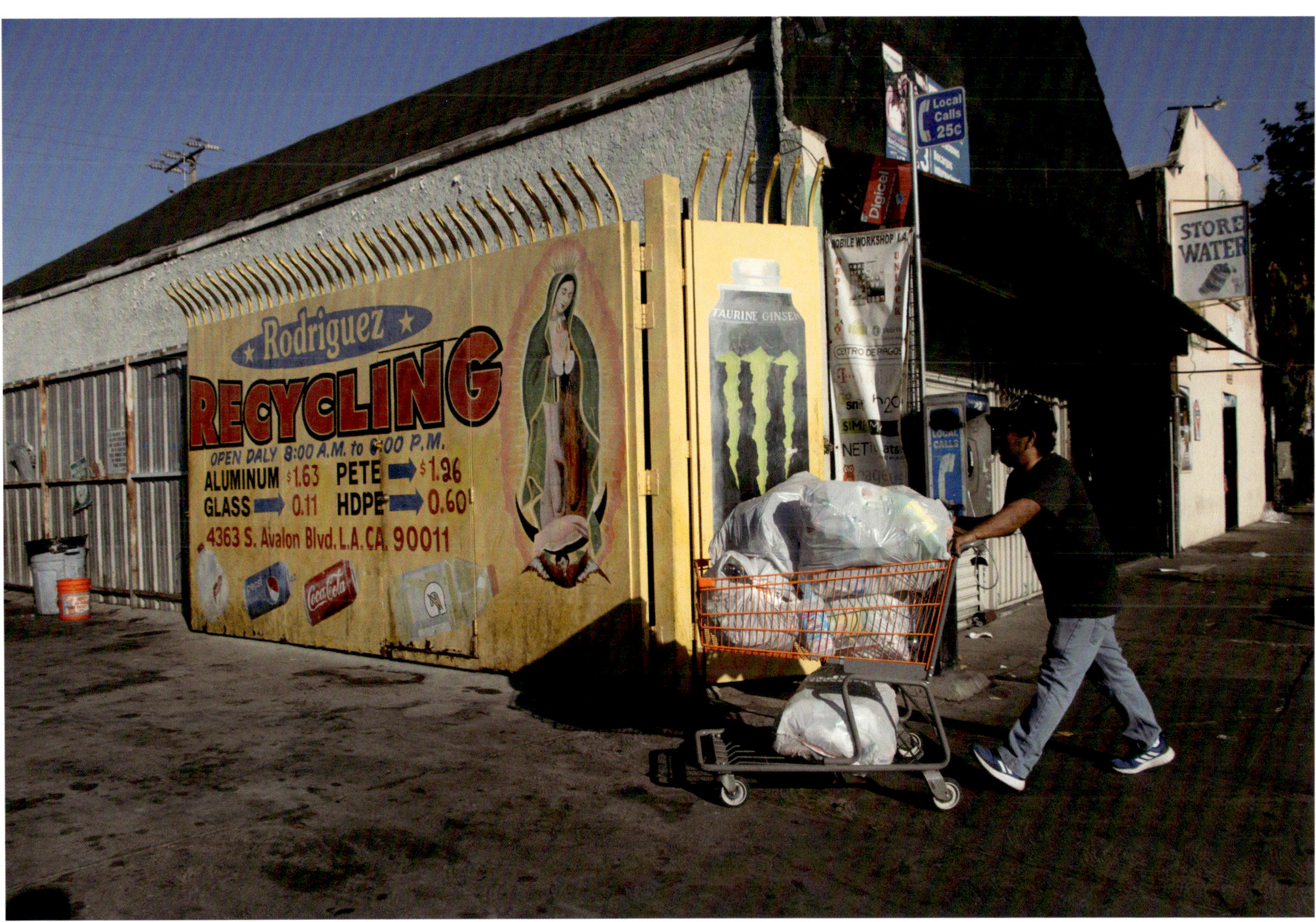
Rodriguez
RECYCLING
OPEN DALY 8:00 A.M. to 6:00 P.M.
ALUMINUM $1.63
PETE $1.26
GLASS 0.11
HDPE 0.60
4363 S. Avalon Blvd. L.A. CA. 90011
Coca-Cola
TAURINE GINSENG
Local Calls 25c
Digicel
MOBILE WORKSHOP L.A.
CENTRO DE PAGOS
STORE WATER

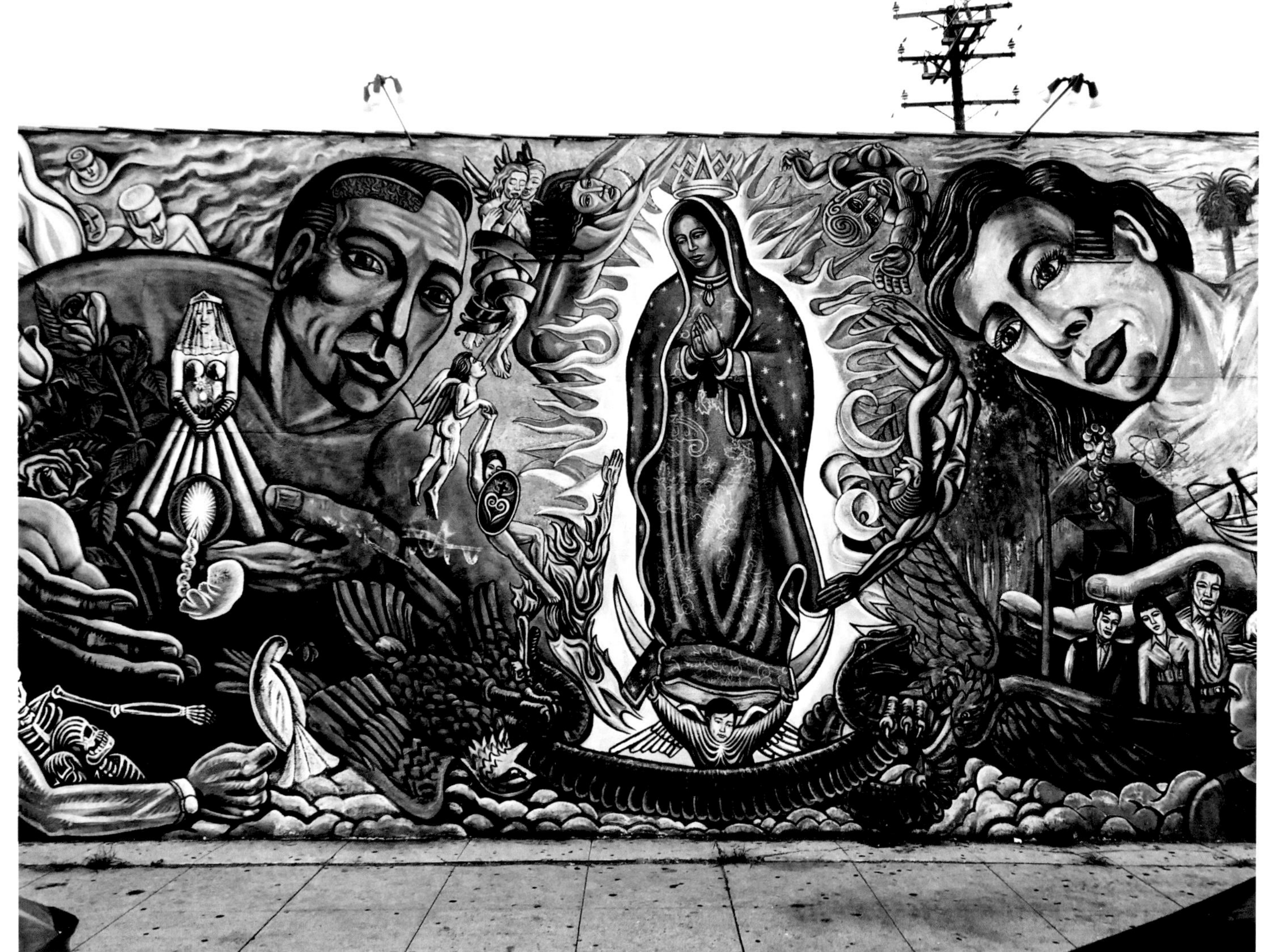

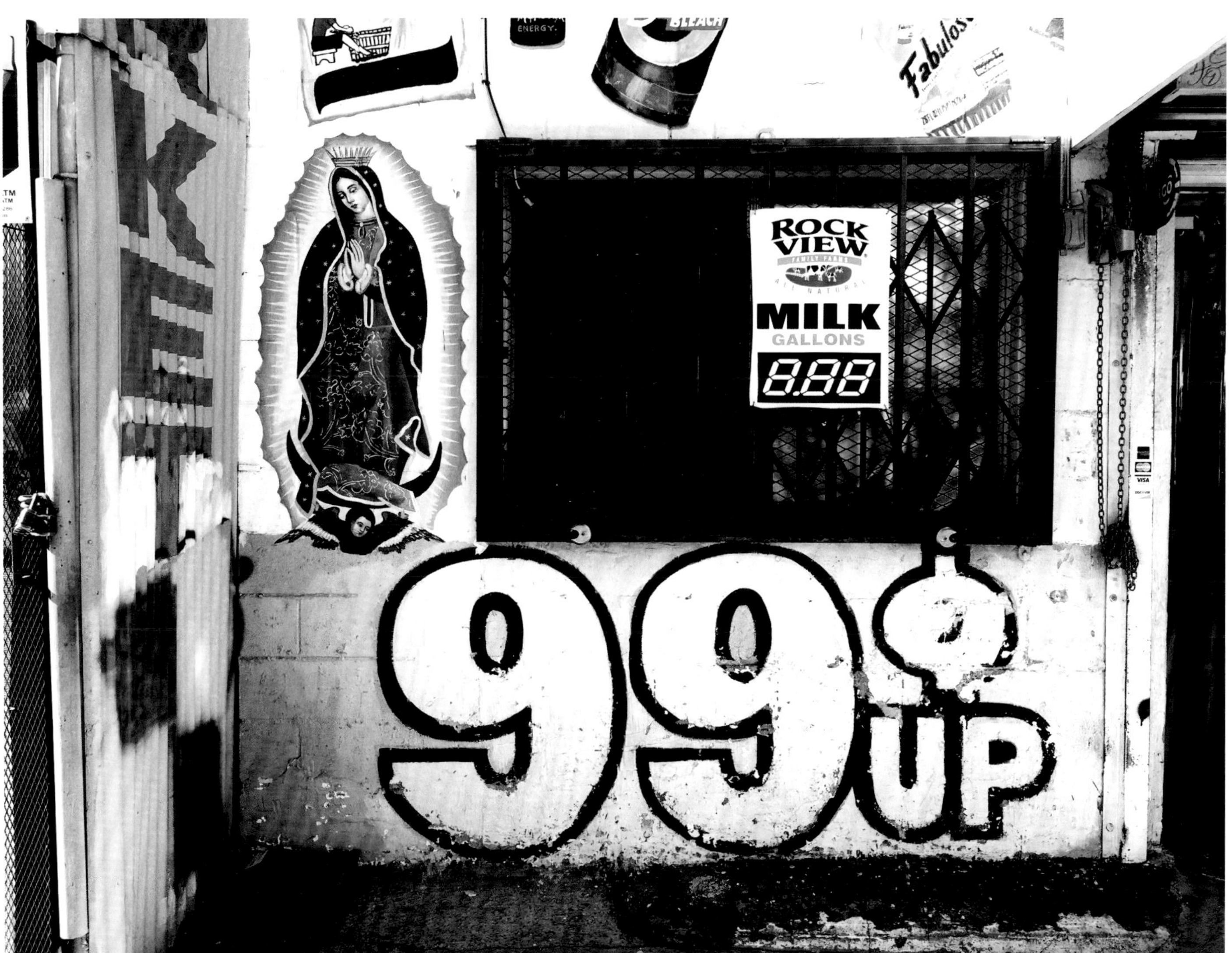
ENERGY.
BLEACH
ROCK VIEW
FAMILY FARMS
ALL NATURAL
MILK
GALLONS
99¢
UP

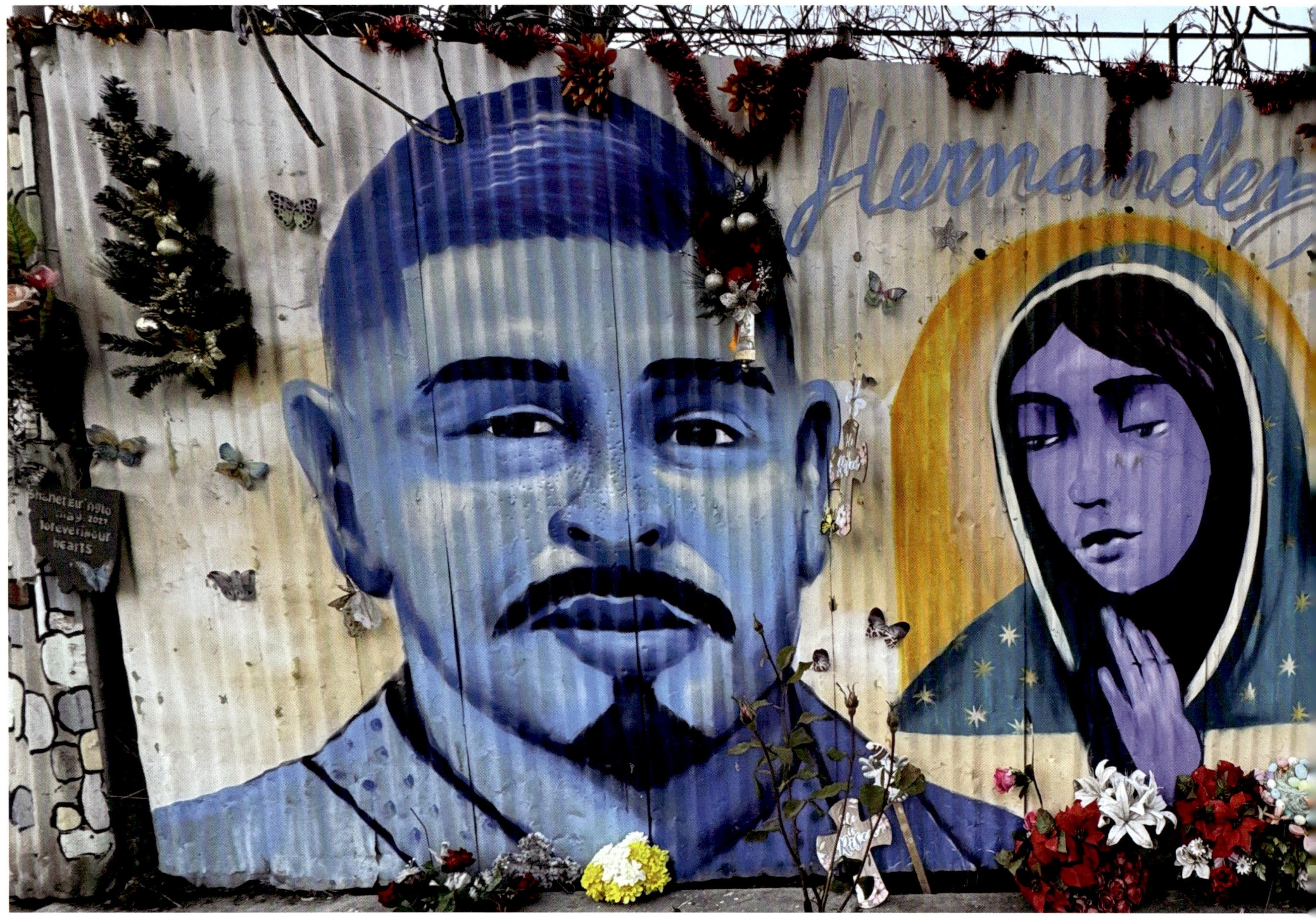
Hernande

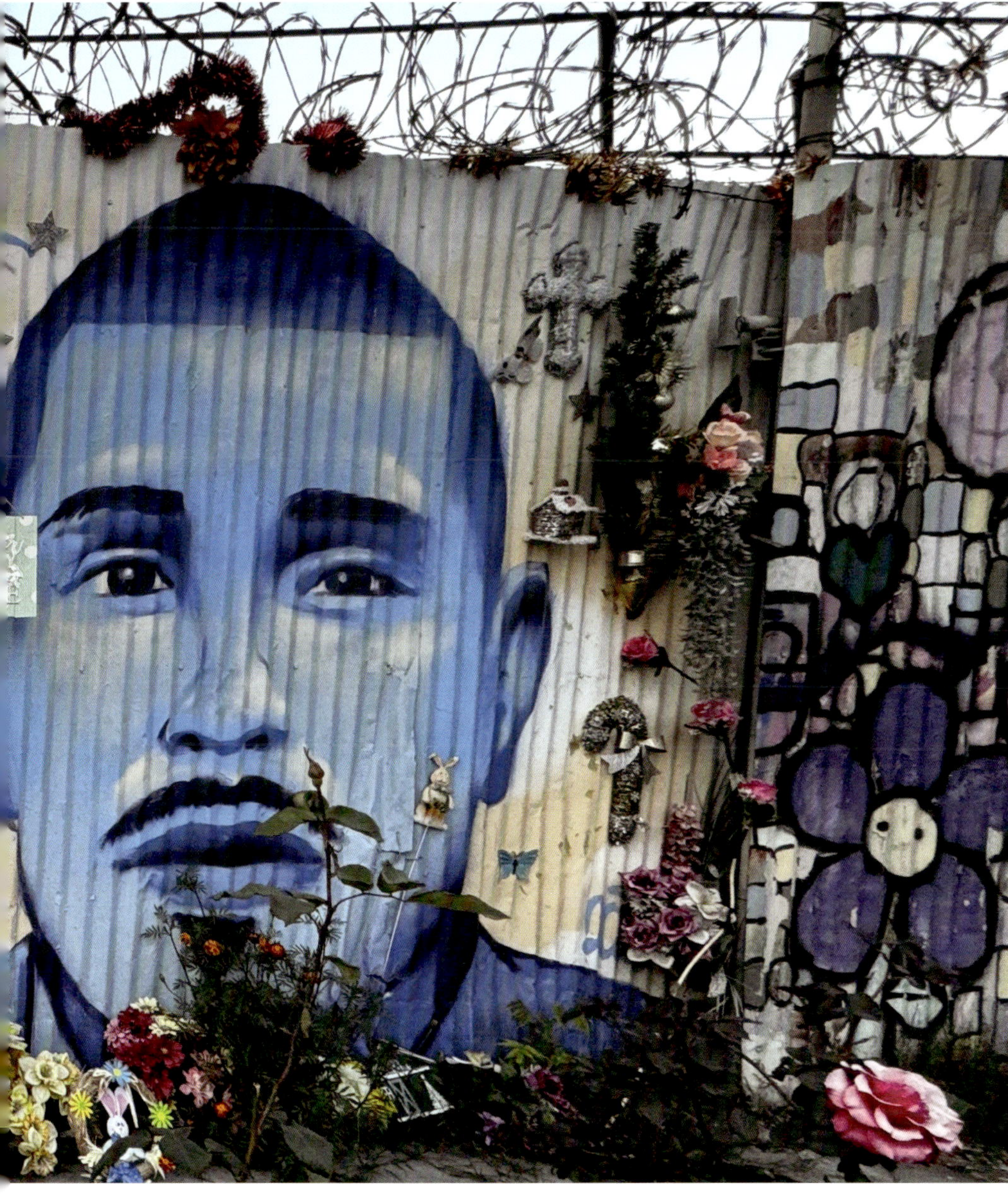

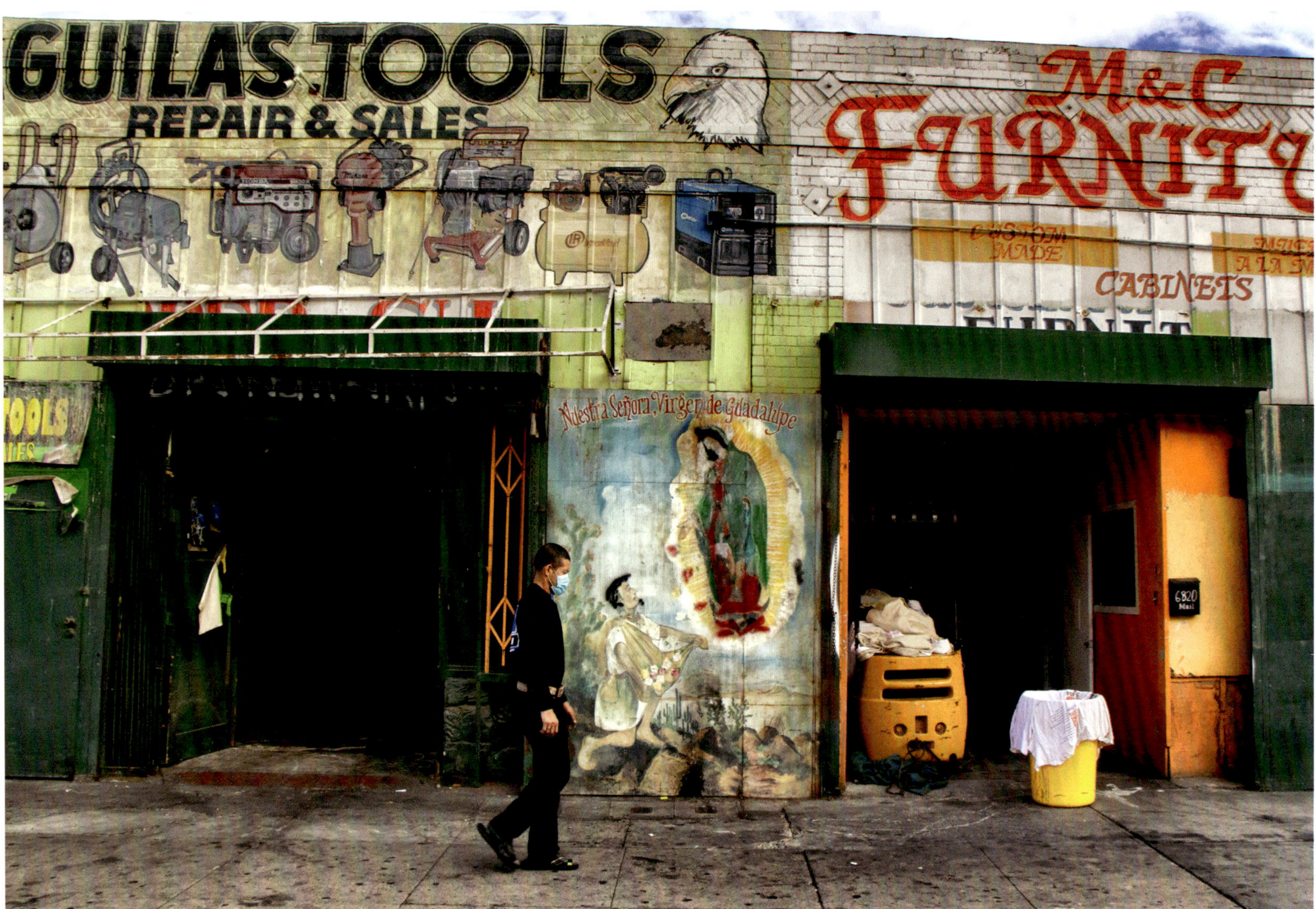
GUILA'S TOOLS
REPAIR & SALES
M&C
FURNIT
CUSTOM MADE
CABINETS
TOOLS
Nuestra Señora, Virgen de Guadalupe
6820
Mail

Migrating from Mexico, both she and they found a home on streets named Hooper, Compton, Slauson, and Whittier.

Migrando desde México, ella, como ellos, encontró un hogar en calles nombradas Hooper, Compton, Slauson, y Whittier.

In recent years, though, gangs have retreated from the public behavior that for so long blighted working-class neighborhoods.

En años recientes, sin embargo, las pandillas han abandonado el comportamiento callejero que por tantos años manchó barrios obreros.

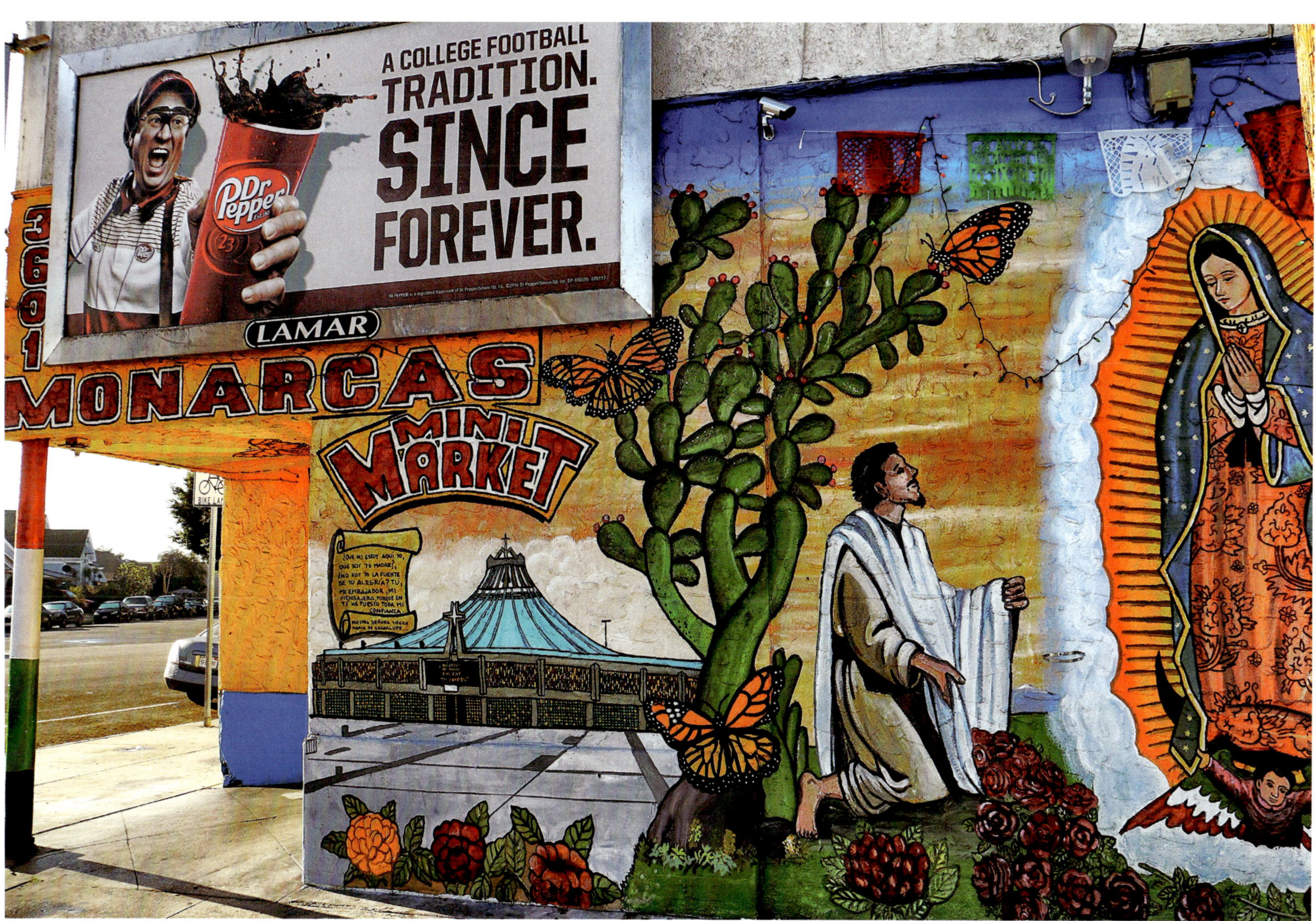
A COLLEGE FOOTBALL
TRADITION.
SINCE
FOREVER.
Dr Pepper
LAMAR
3601
MONARCAS
MINI MARKET
¿QUE NO ESTOY AQUÍ YO,
QUE SOY TU MADRE?,
¿NO SOY YO LA FUENTE
DE TU ALEGRÍA? TÚ,
MI EMBAJADOR, MI
MENSAJERO, PORQUE EN
TI HE PUESTO TODA MI
CONFIANZA.
NUESTRA SEÑORA VIRGEN
MARIA DE GUADALUPE.

Property values are climbing.

Los valores de bienes raíces están en aumento.

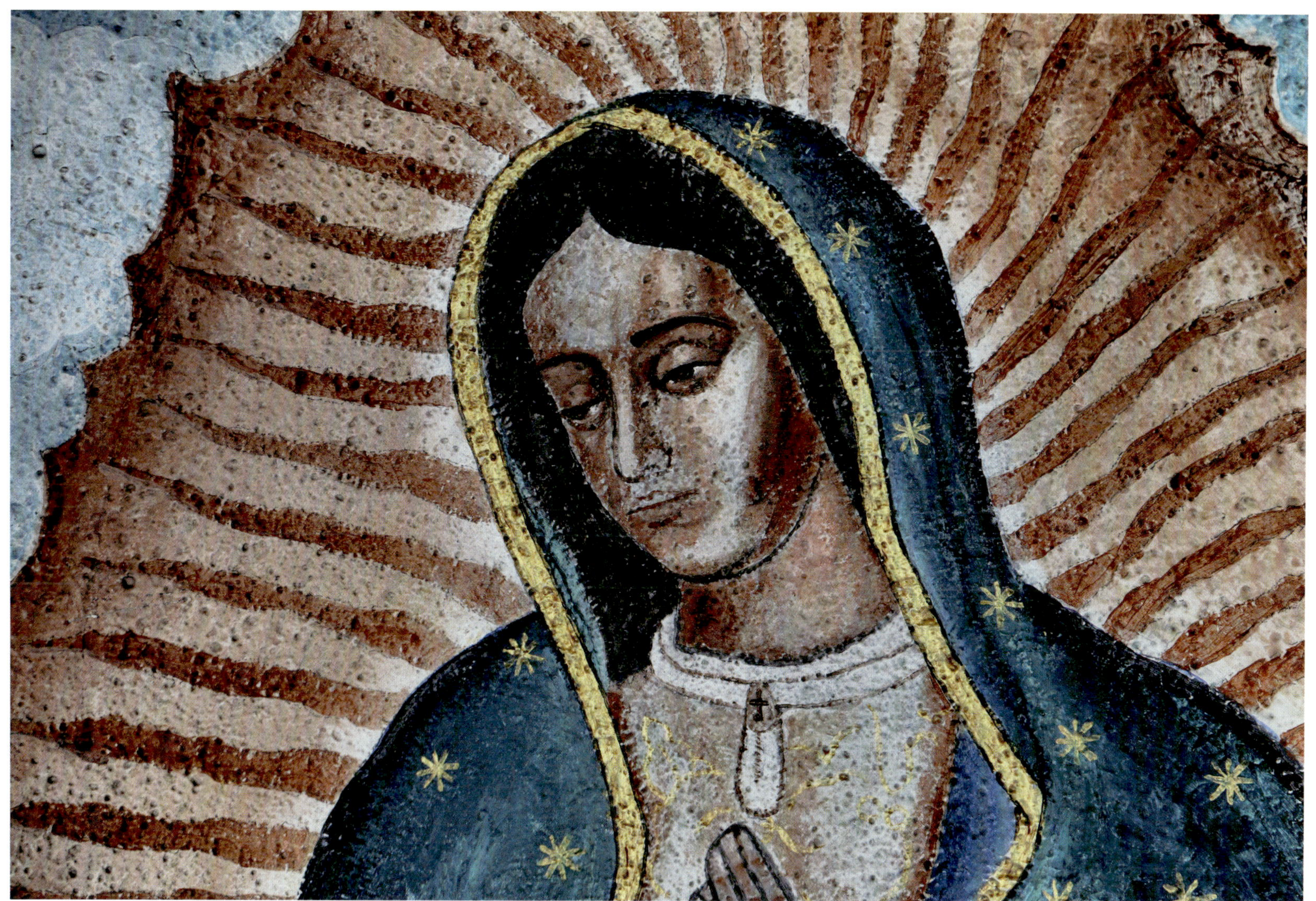

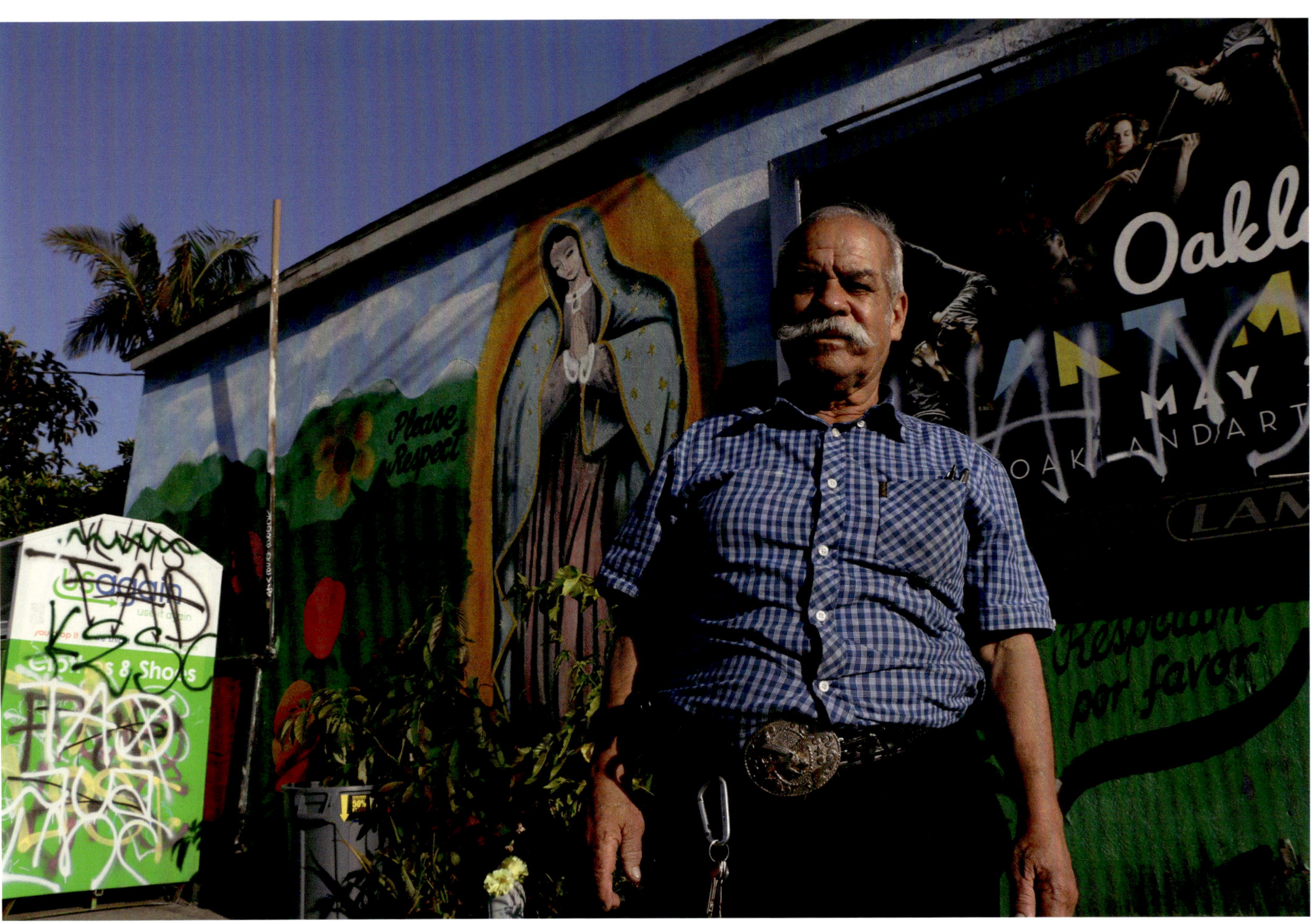
Please Respect
MAY
por favor

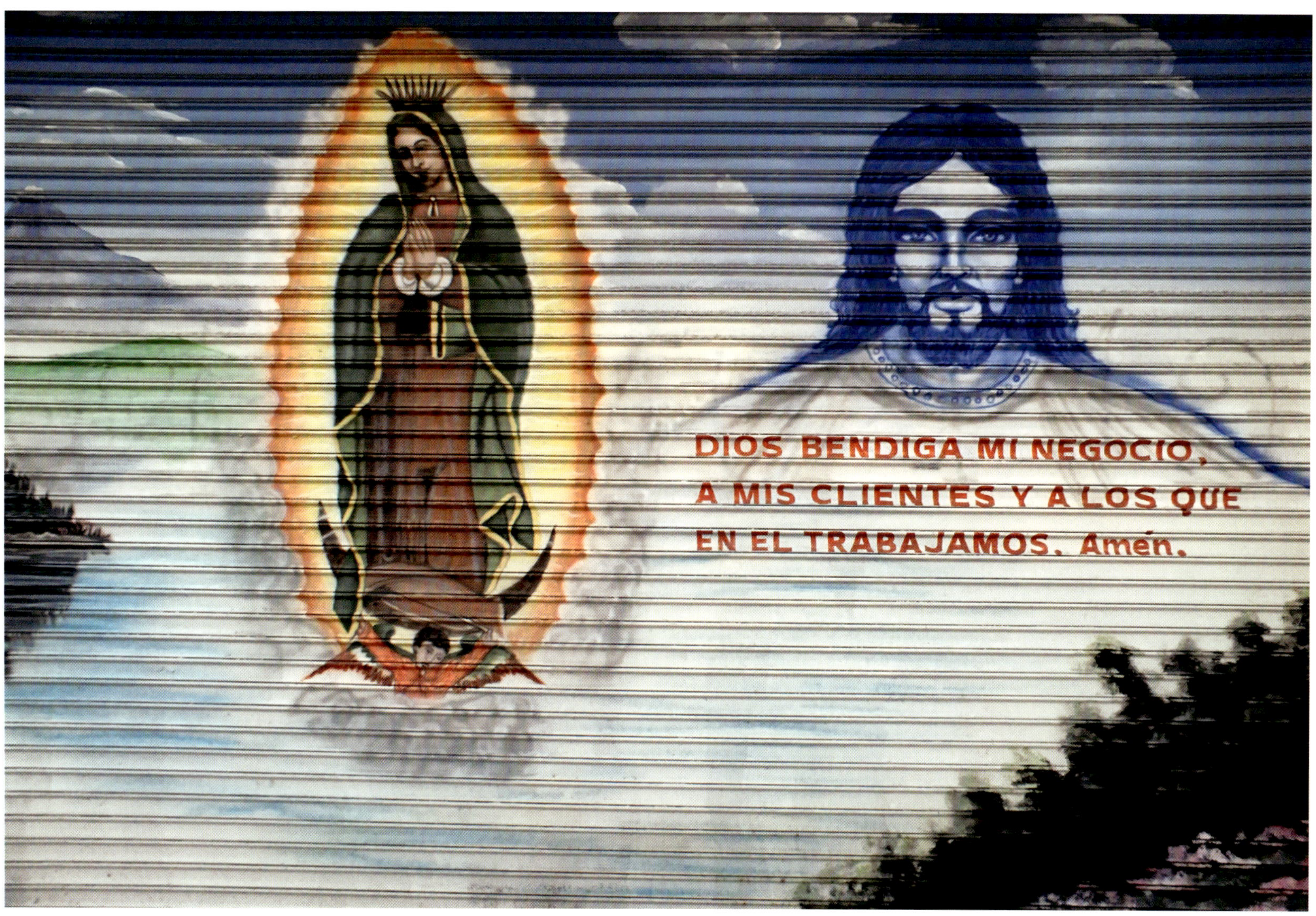
DIOS BENDIGA MI NEGOCIO,
A MIS CLIENTES Y A LOS QUE
EN EL TRABAJAMOS. Amén.

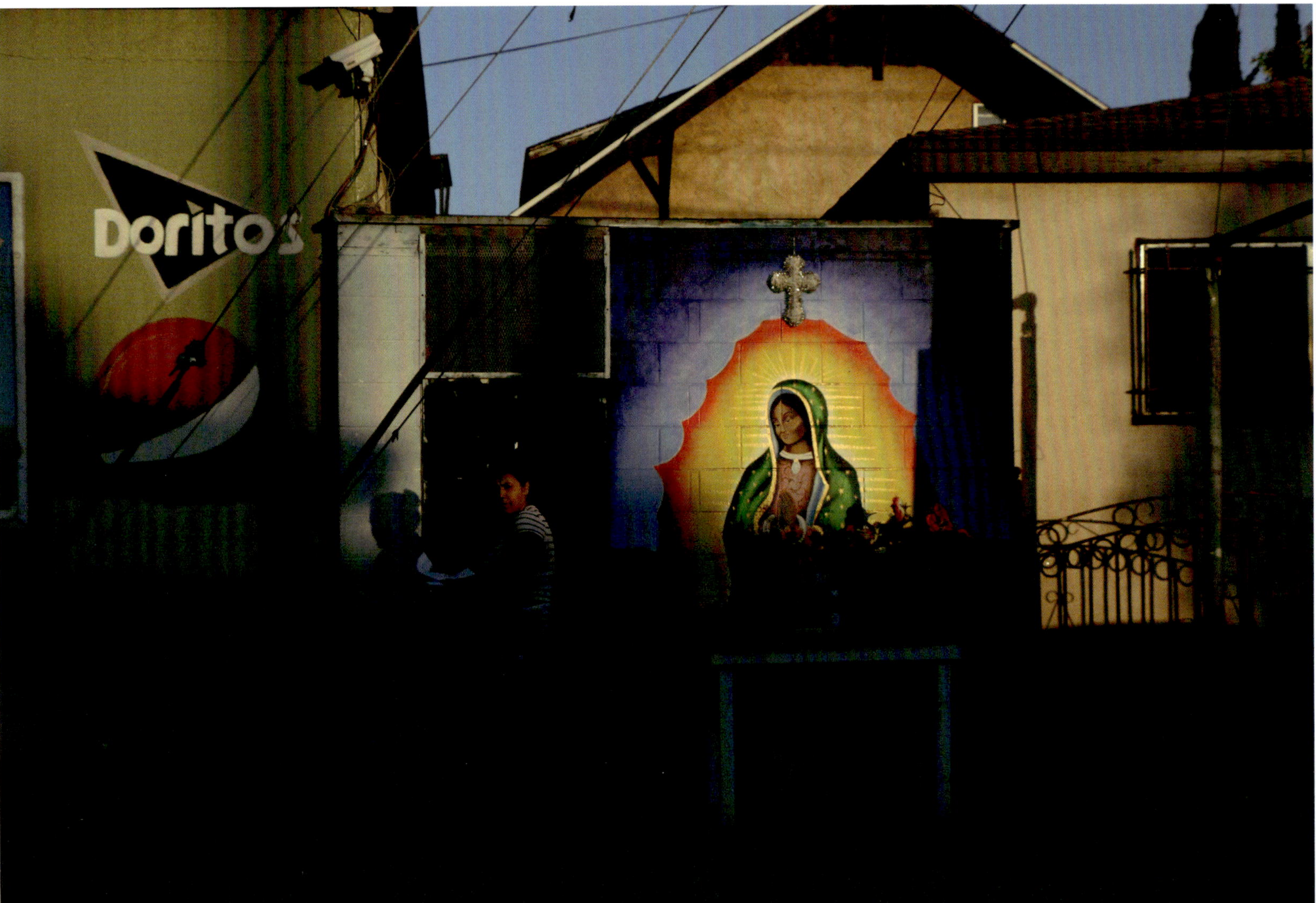
Doritos

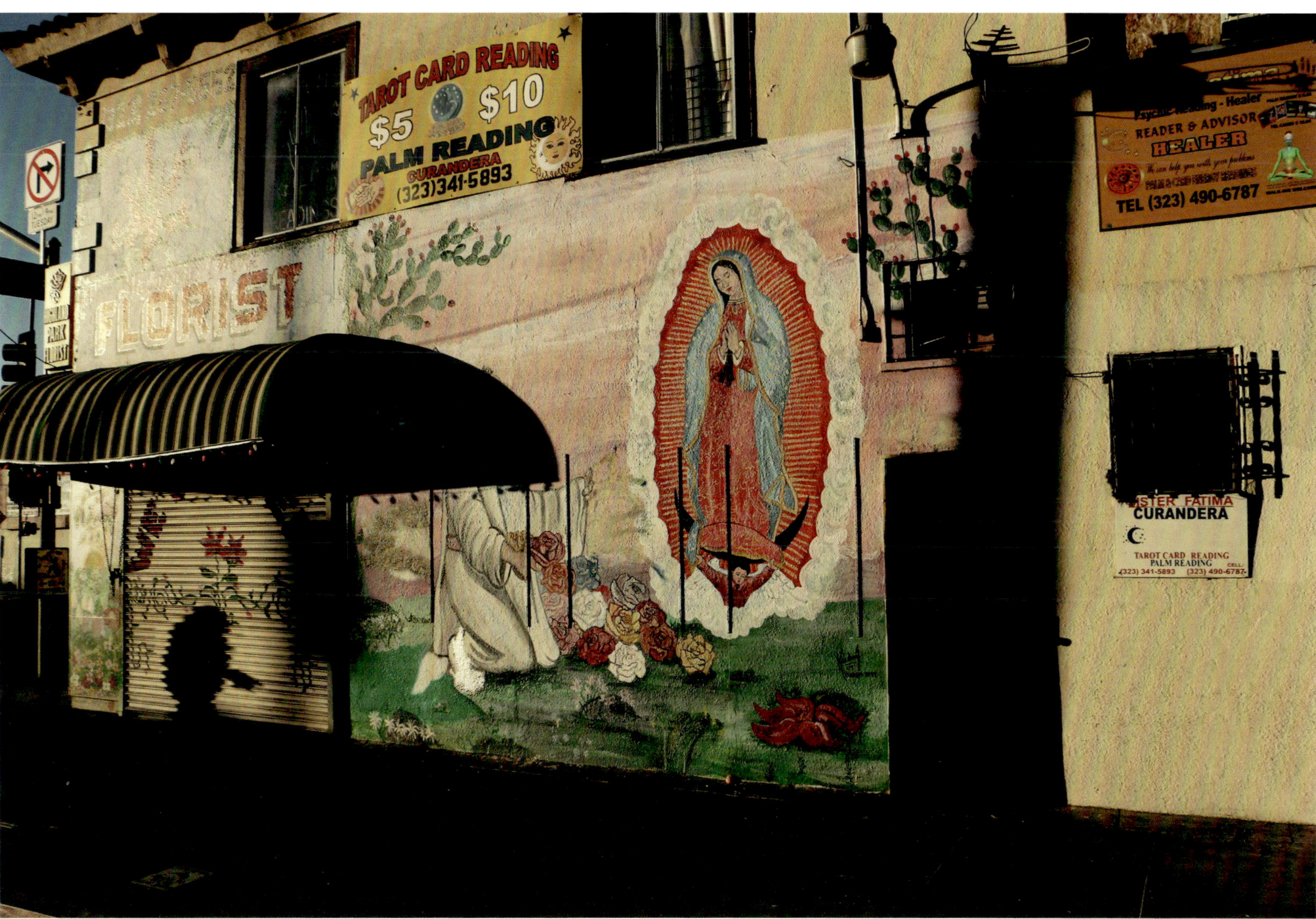
TAROT CARD READING
$5
$10
PALM READING
CURANDERA
(323)341-5893
FLORIST
READER & ADVISOR
HEALER
TEL (323) 490-6787
CURANDERA
TAROT CARD READING
PALM READING
(323) 341-5893
(323) 490-6787

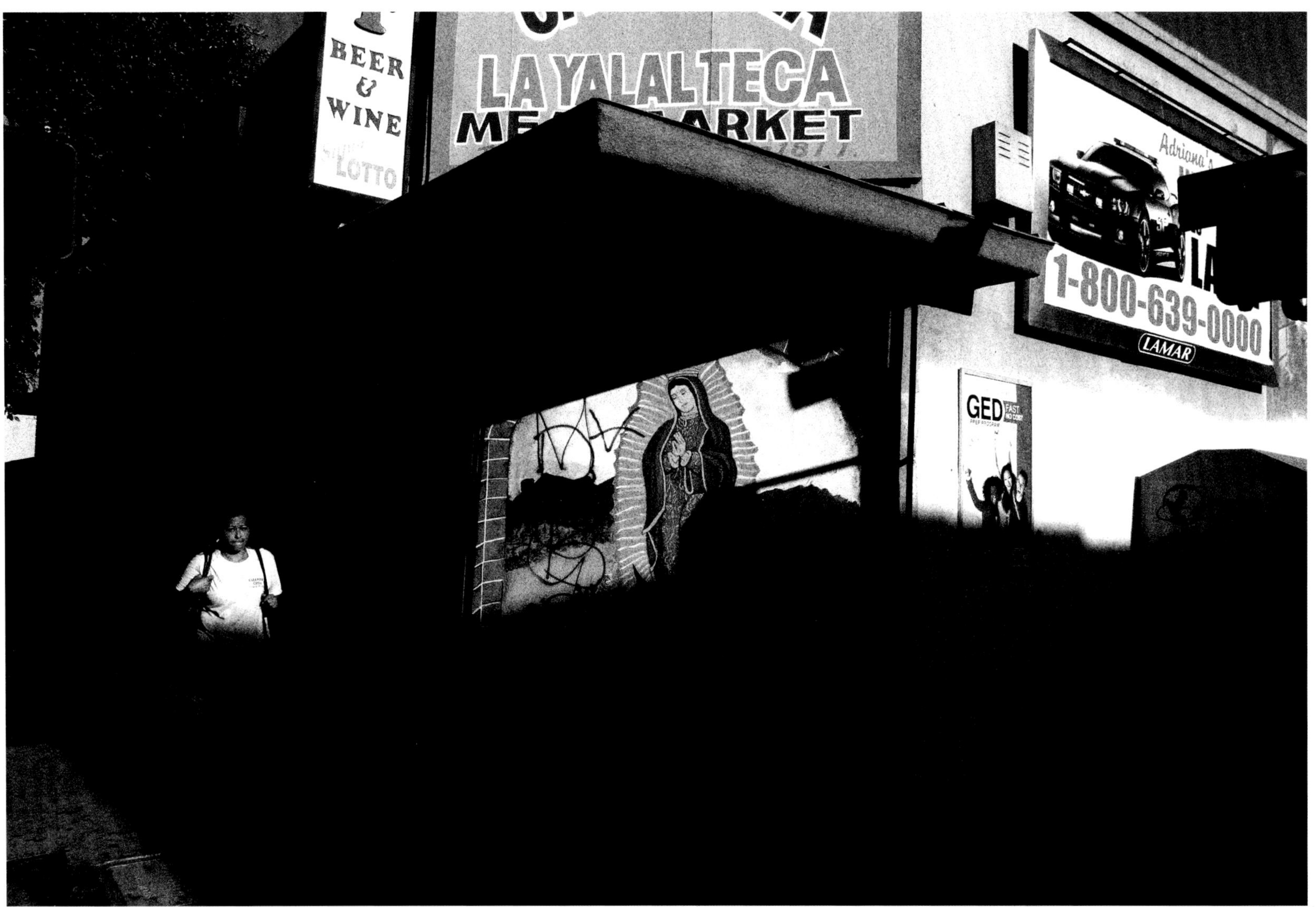
BEER
&
WINE
LOTTO
LA YALALTECA
Adriana's
1-800-639-0000
LAMAR
GED

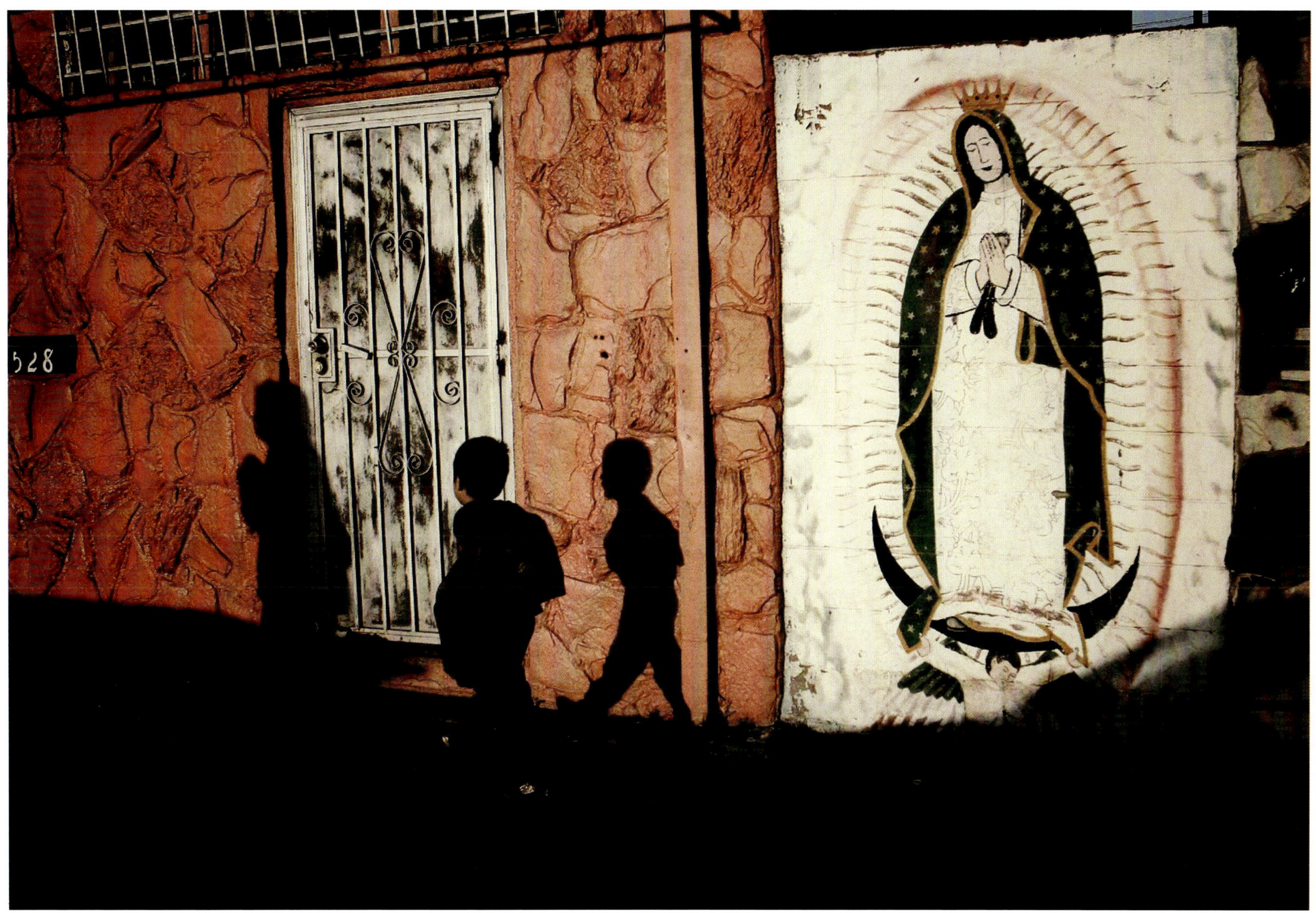
528

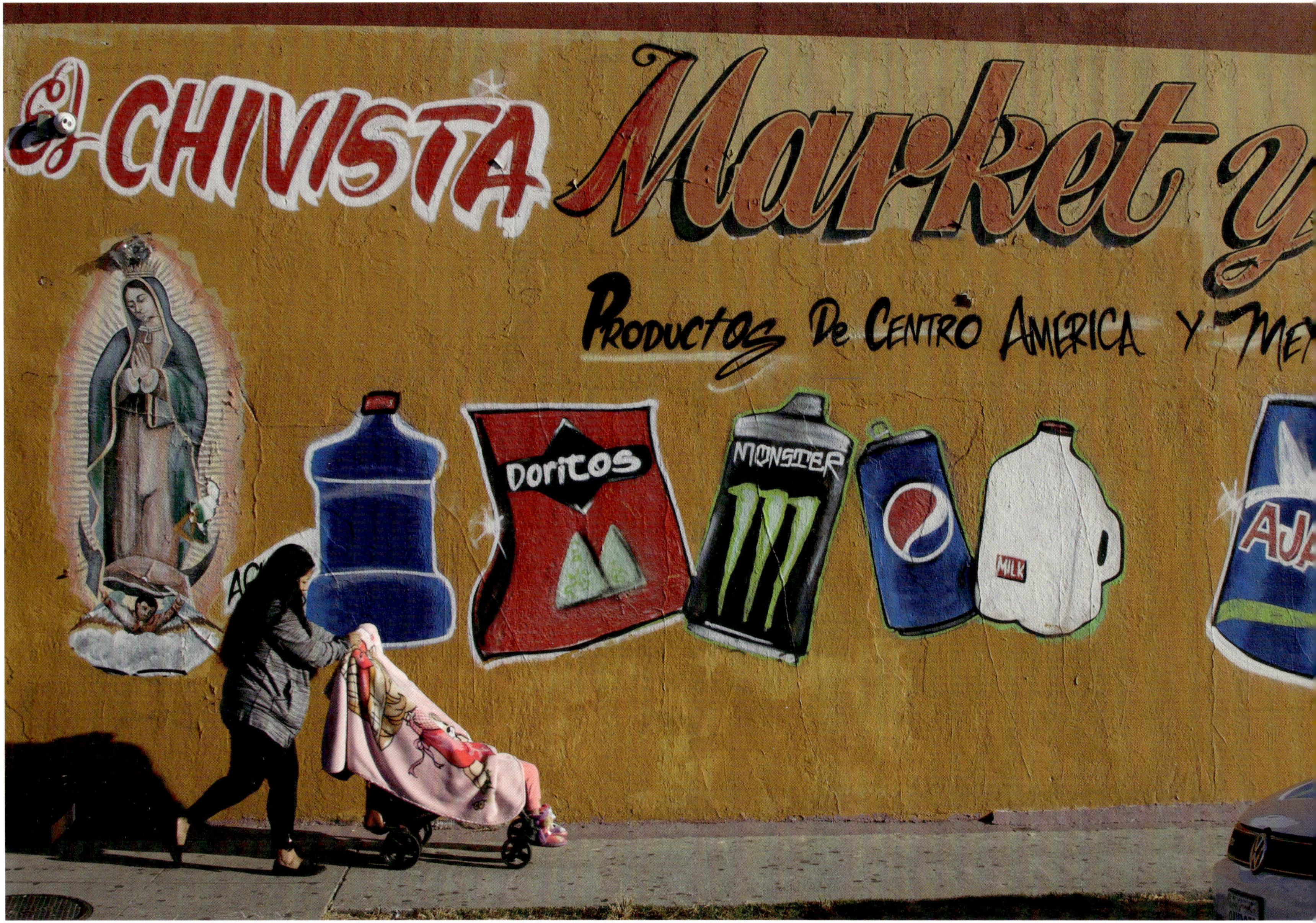

El CHIVISTA Market
Productos De Centro America
Doritos
MONSTER
MILK

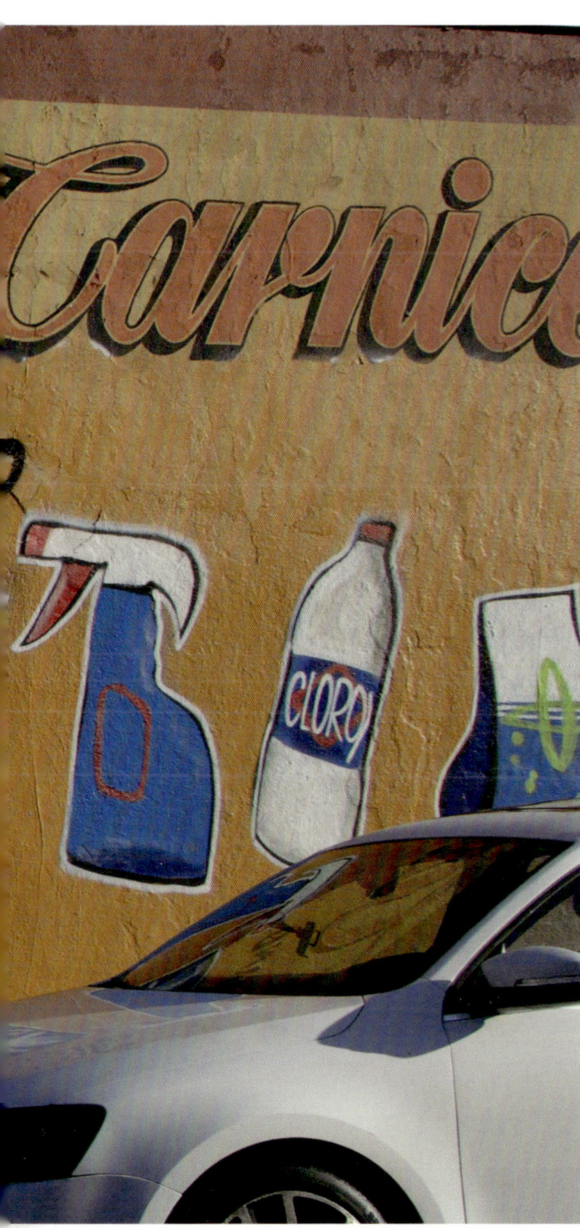

Some barrios that the Virgin once graced are no longer such isolated enclaves of Mexican culture.

Algunos barrios donde la Virgen apareció ya no son los enclaves tan aislados de la cultura mexicana que fueron por tantos años.

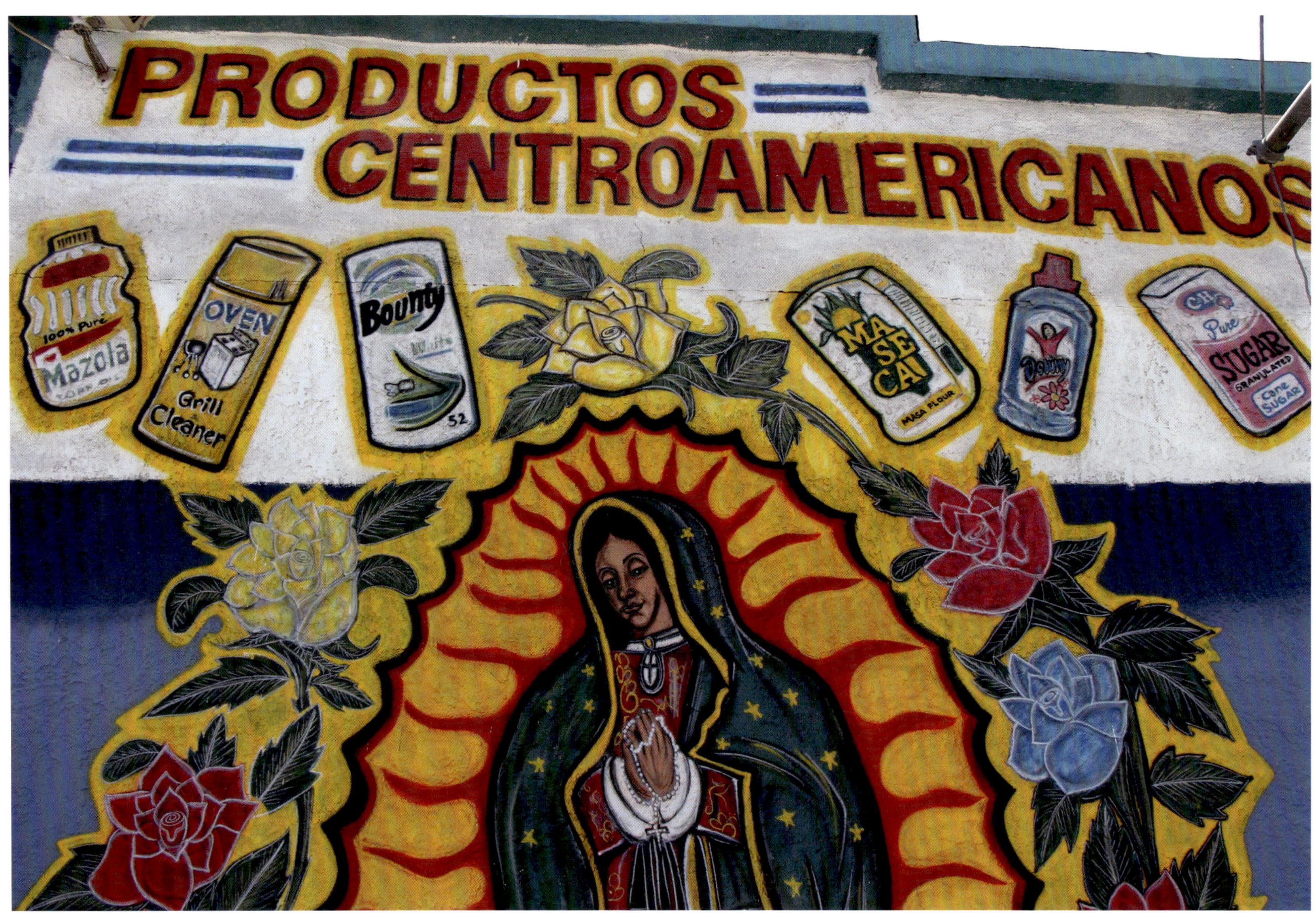
PRODUCTOS
CENTROAMERICANOS
100% Pure
Mazola
OVEN
Grill
Cleaner
Bounty
52
MA
SE
CA
MASA FLOUR
Downy
Pure
SUGAR
GRANULATED
Cane
SUGAR

Some of her murals have disappeared after their businesses were replaced by a 7-Eleven or a Subway sandwich shop.

Algunos de sus murales han desaparecido después de que sus negocios fueron reemplazados por un 7-Eleven o un Subway.

Meanwhile, taggers don't have the reverence for her that gang members once had.

Mientras tanto, los taggers *parecen haber perdido la reverencia por ella que los pandilleros le tuvieron por años.*

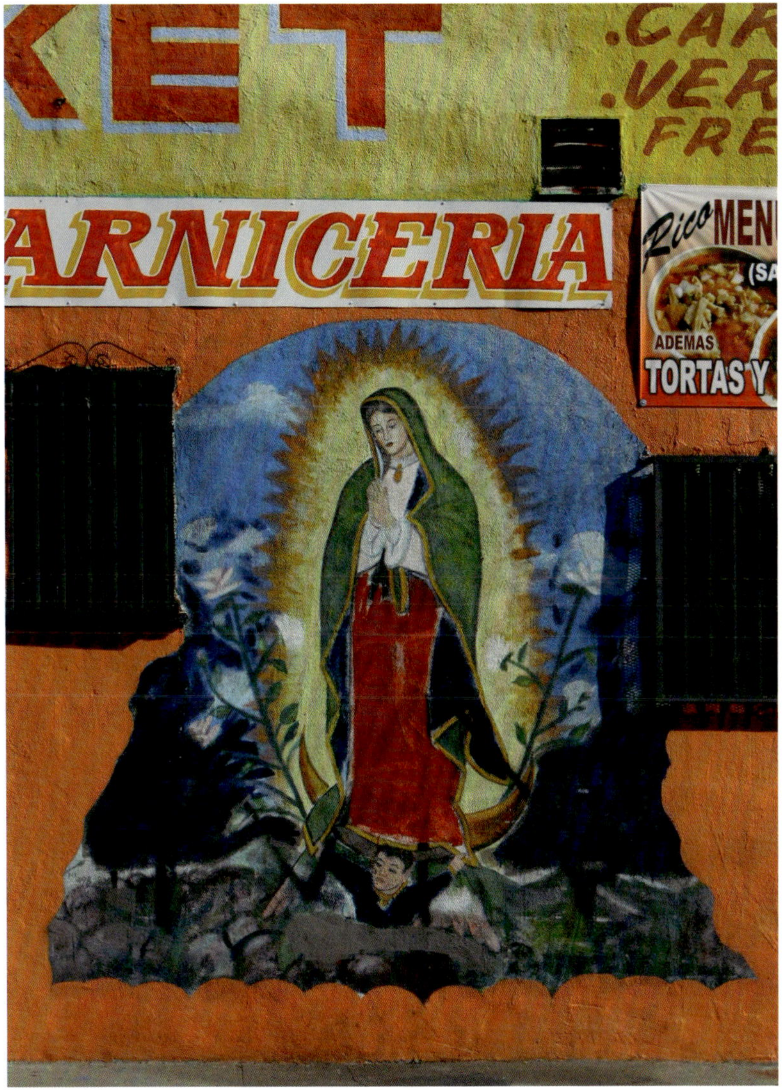

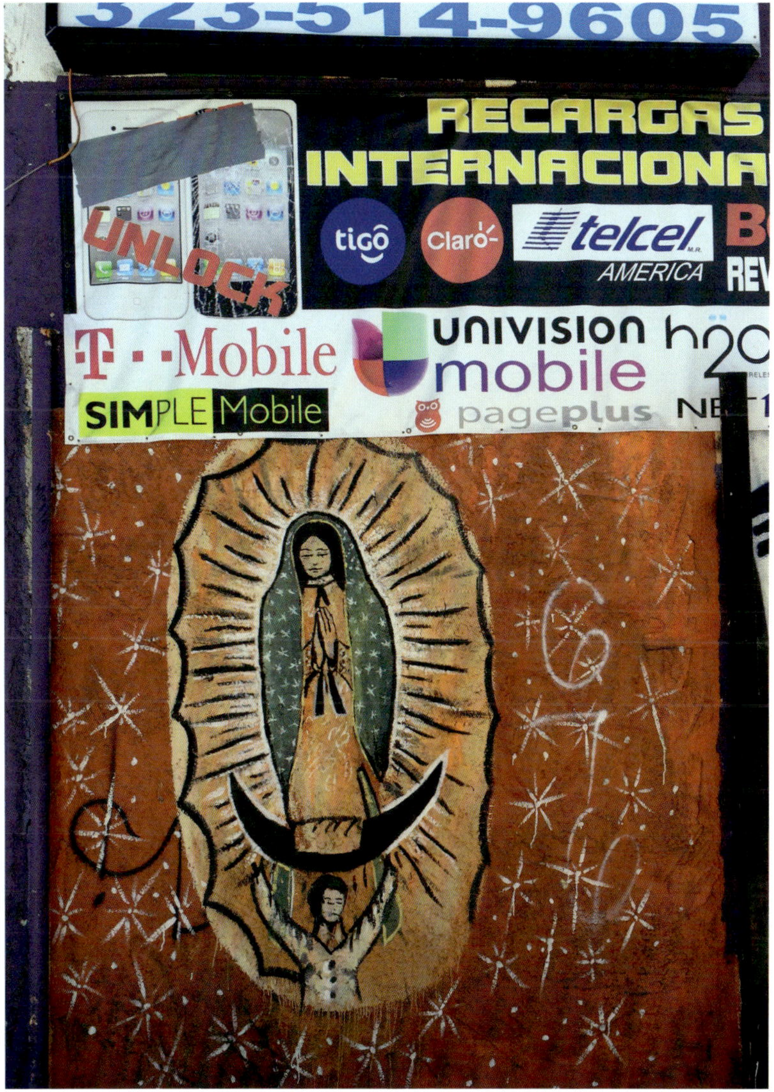

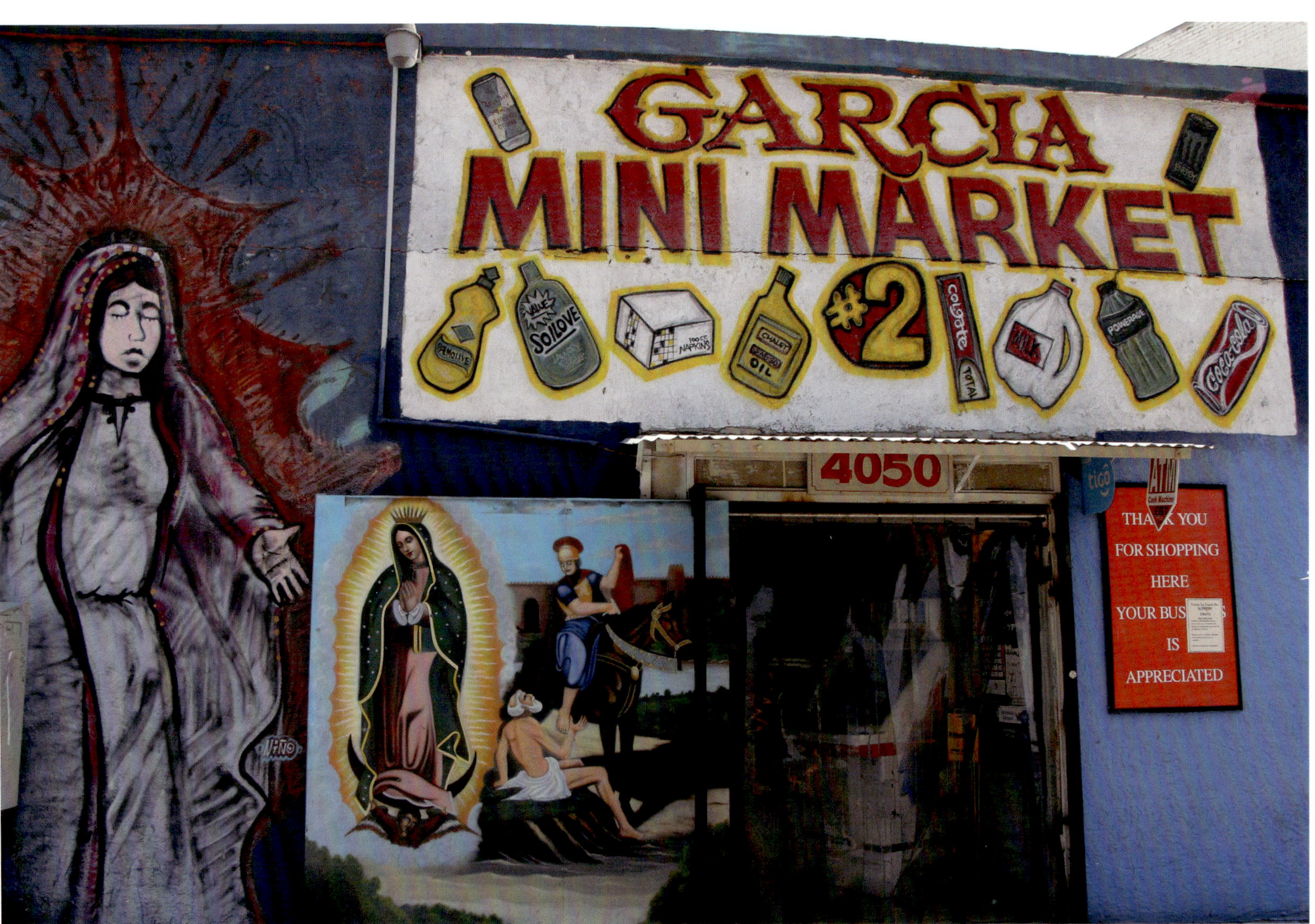

GARCIA
MINI MARKET
#2
4050
THANK YOU
FOR SHOPPING
HERE
YOUR BUSINESS
IS
APPRECIATED

And fewer new murals of the Virgin are going up on the walls of Los Angeles.

Y menos murales de la Virgen se están pintando en las paredes de Los Ángeles.

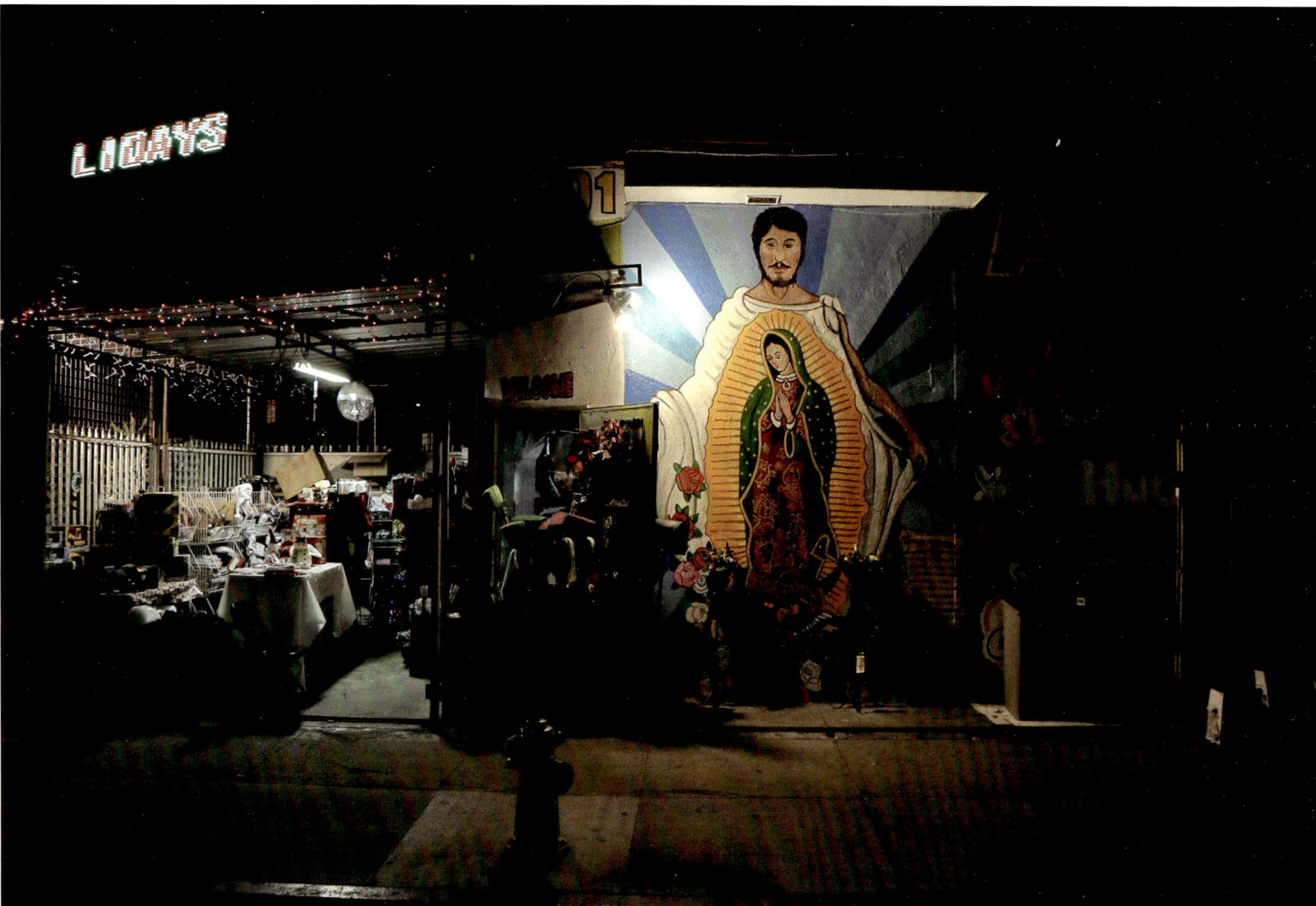
LIDAYS

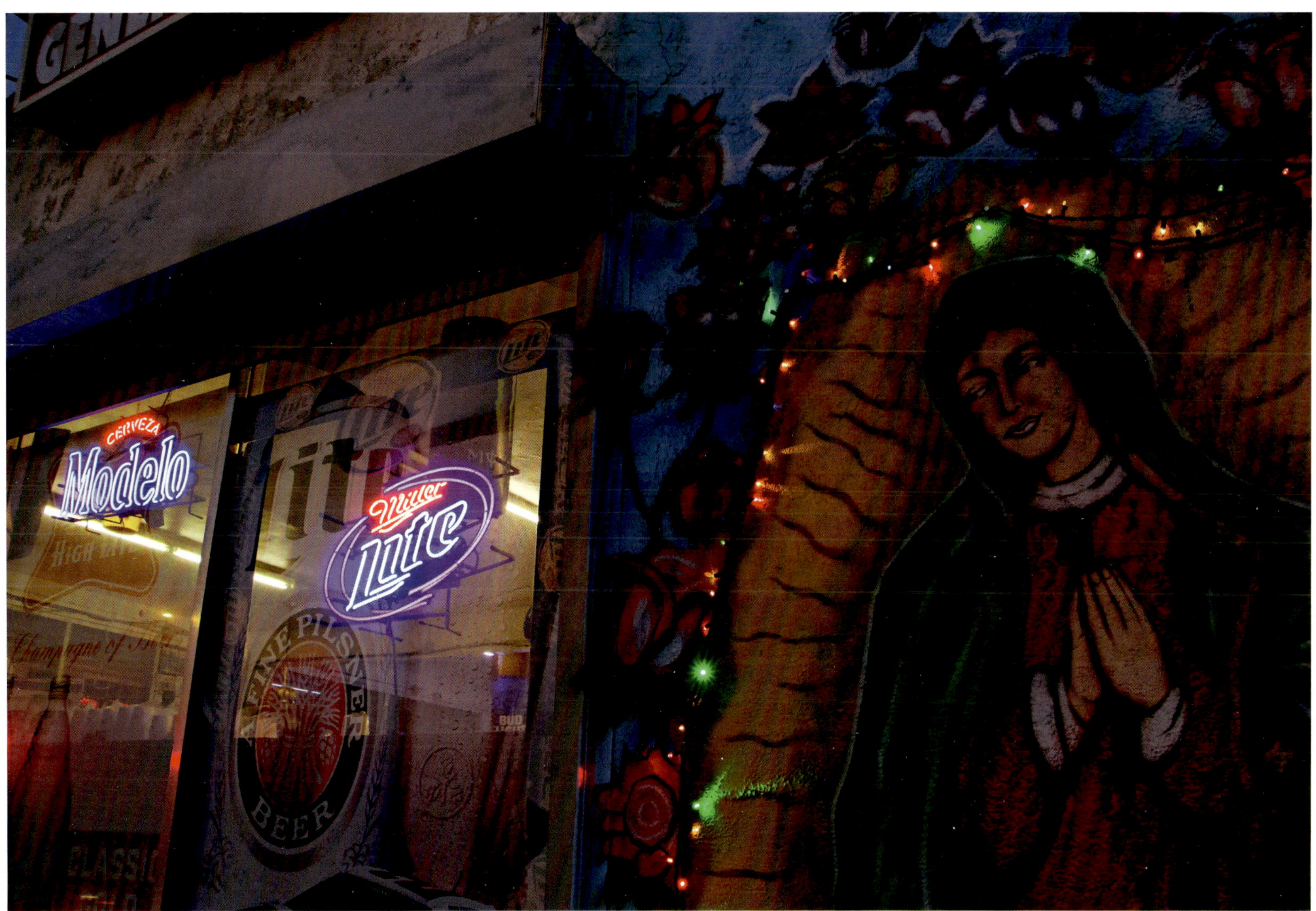
CERVEZA
Modelo
Miller
Lite
A FINE PILSNER
BEER
CLASSIC

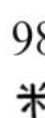

Yet though she may not be present as often as in the past,

Sin embargo, aunque quizás no esté presente tanto como antes,

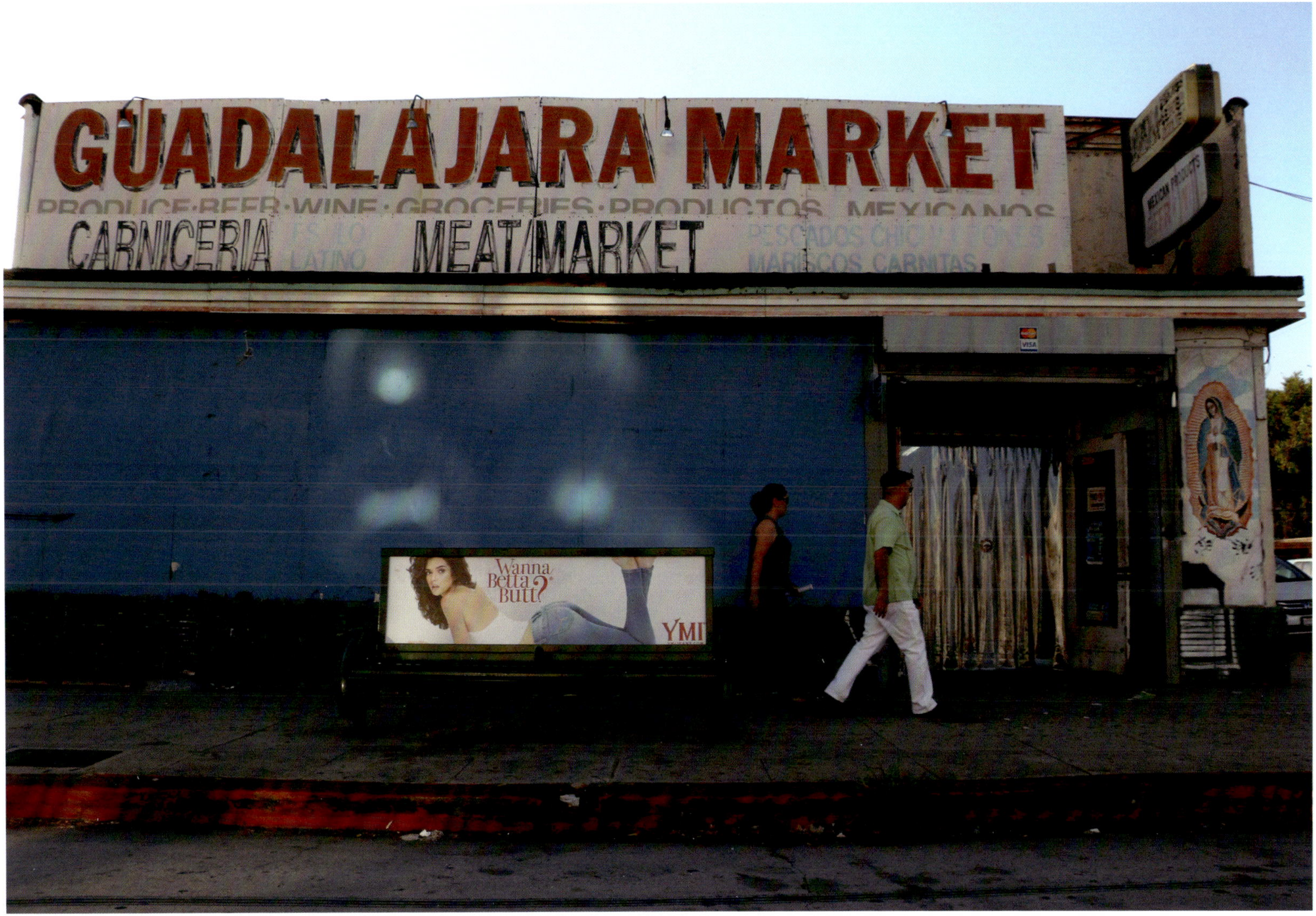

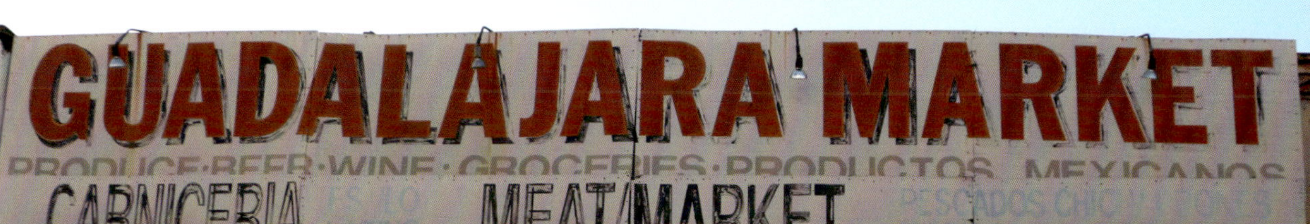
GUADALAJARA MARKET
PRODUCE·BEER·WINE·GROCERIES·PRODUCTOS MEXICANOS
CARNICERIA
MEAT/MARKET
MARISCOS CARNITAS

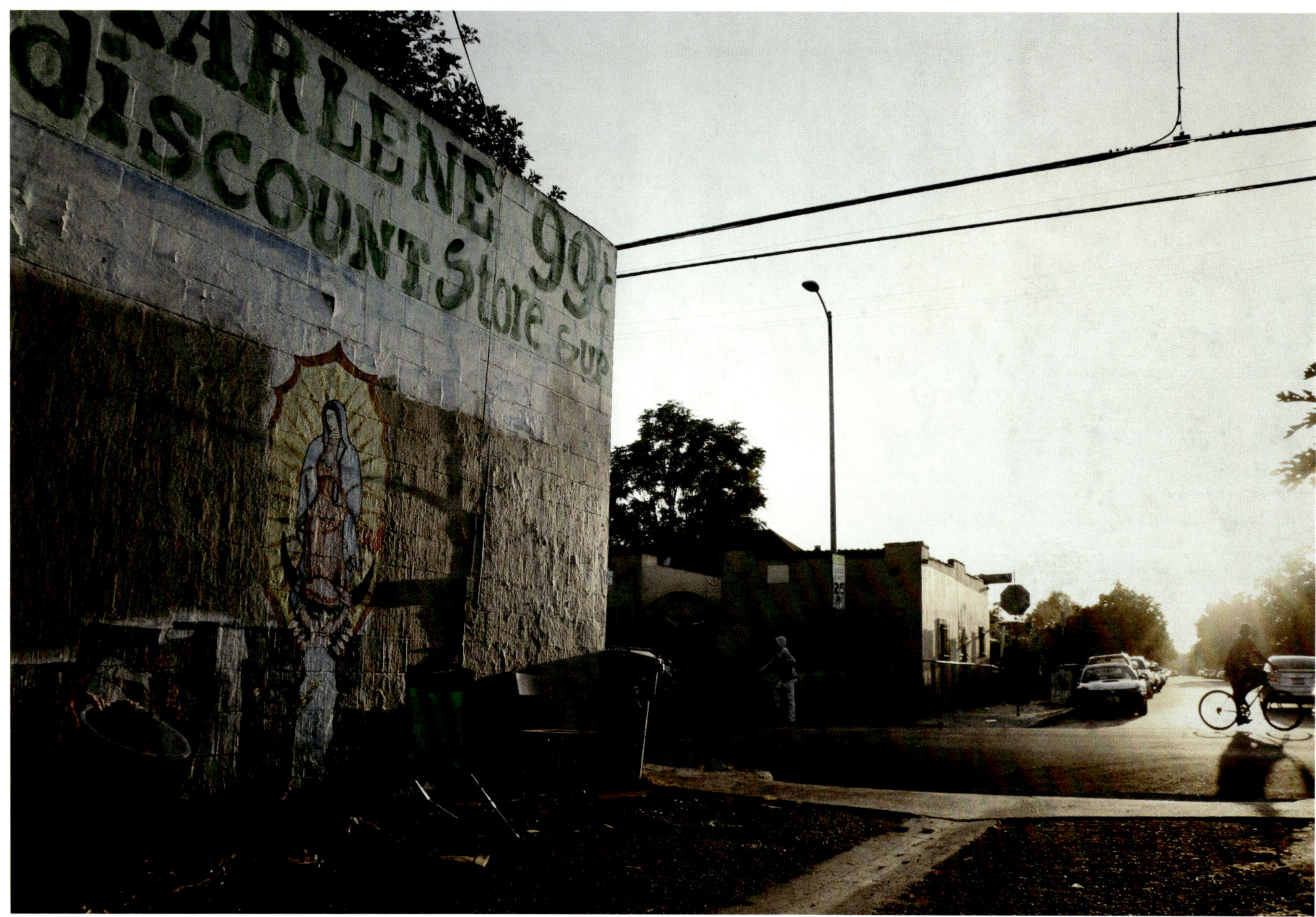
ARLENE 99¢
DISCOUNT Store SUP

it's comforting to know that from the walls of many markets, car washes, and flower shops…

nos da confort saber que desde mercados, desde los car wash *y desde las florerías…*

she smiles down on us still…

nos sonríe a todos nosotros todavía

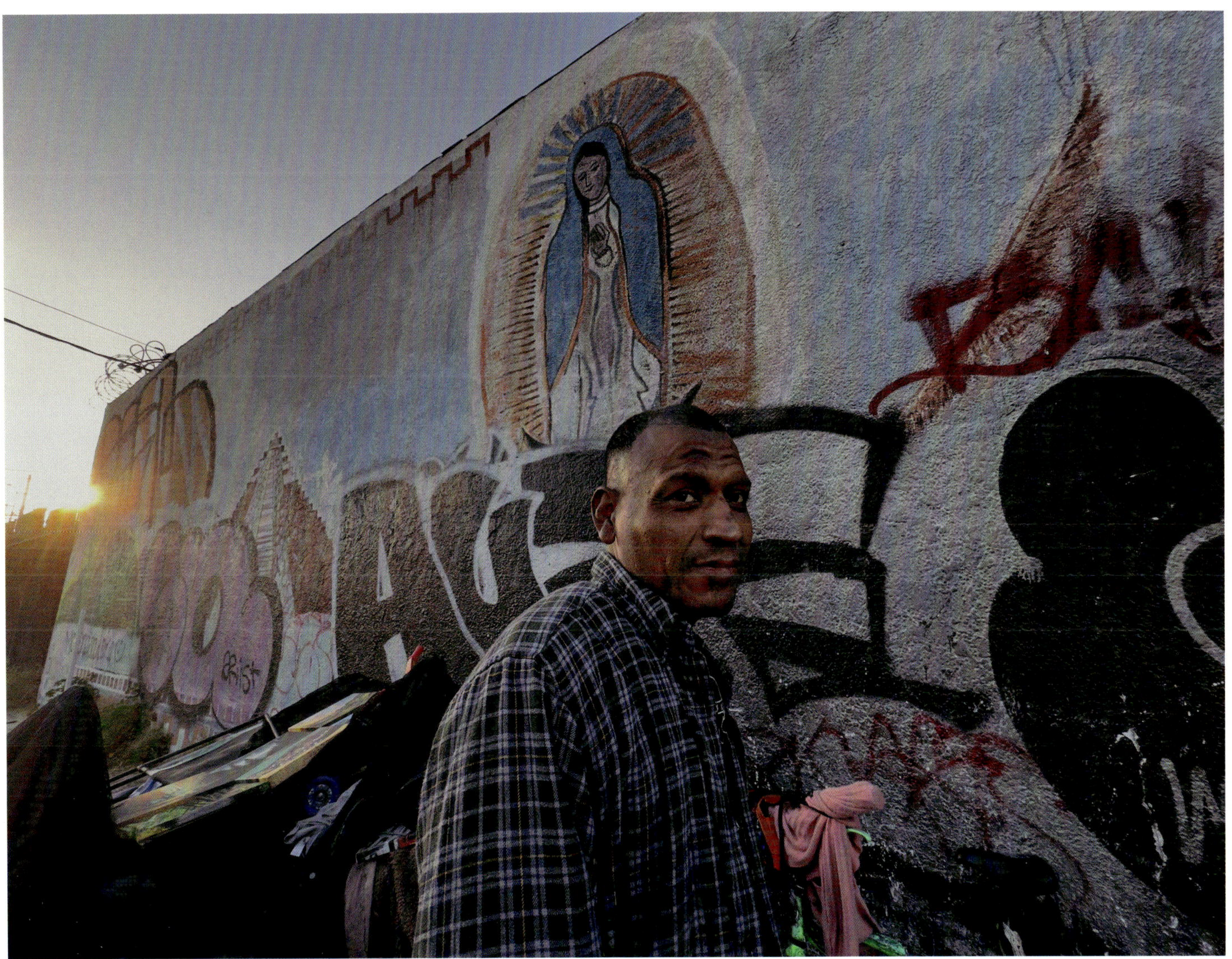

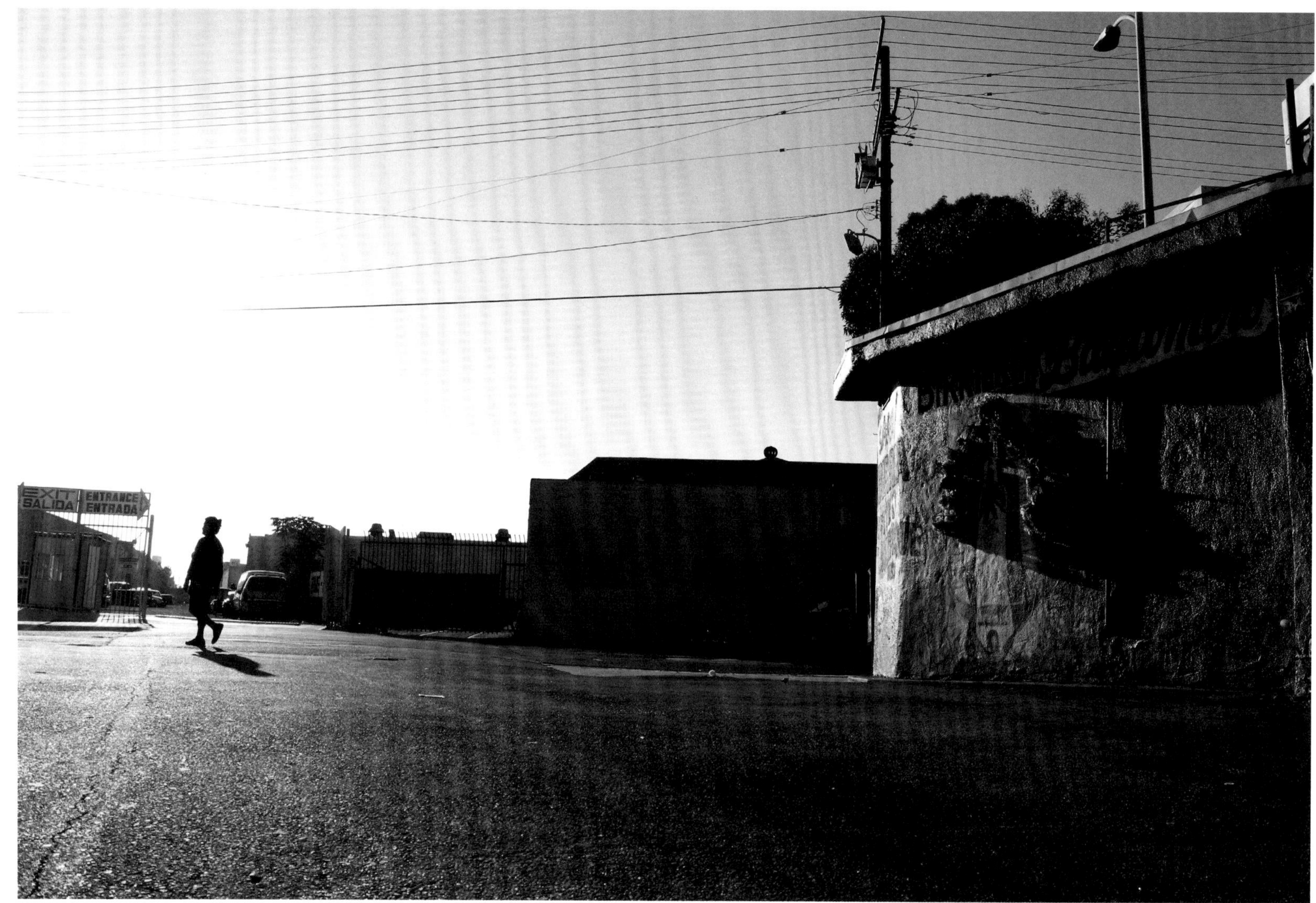
EXIT
SALIDA
ENTRANCE
ENTRADA

…patiently, quietly,

…pacientemente, silenciosamente

there when we need her.

allí cuando la necesitamos.

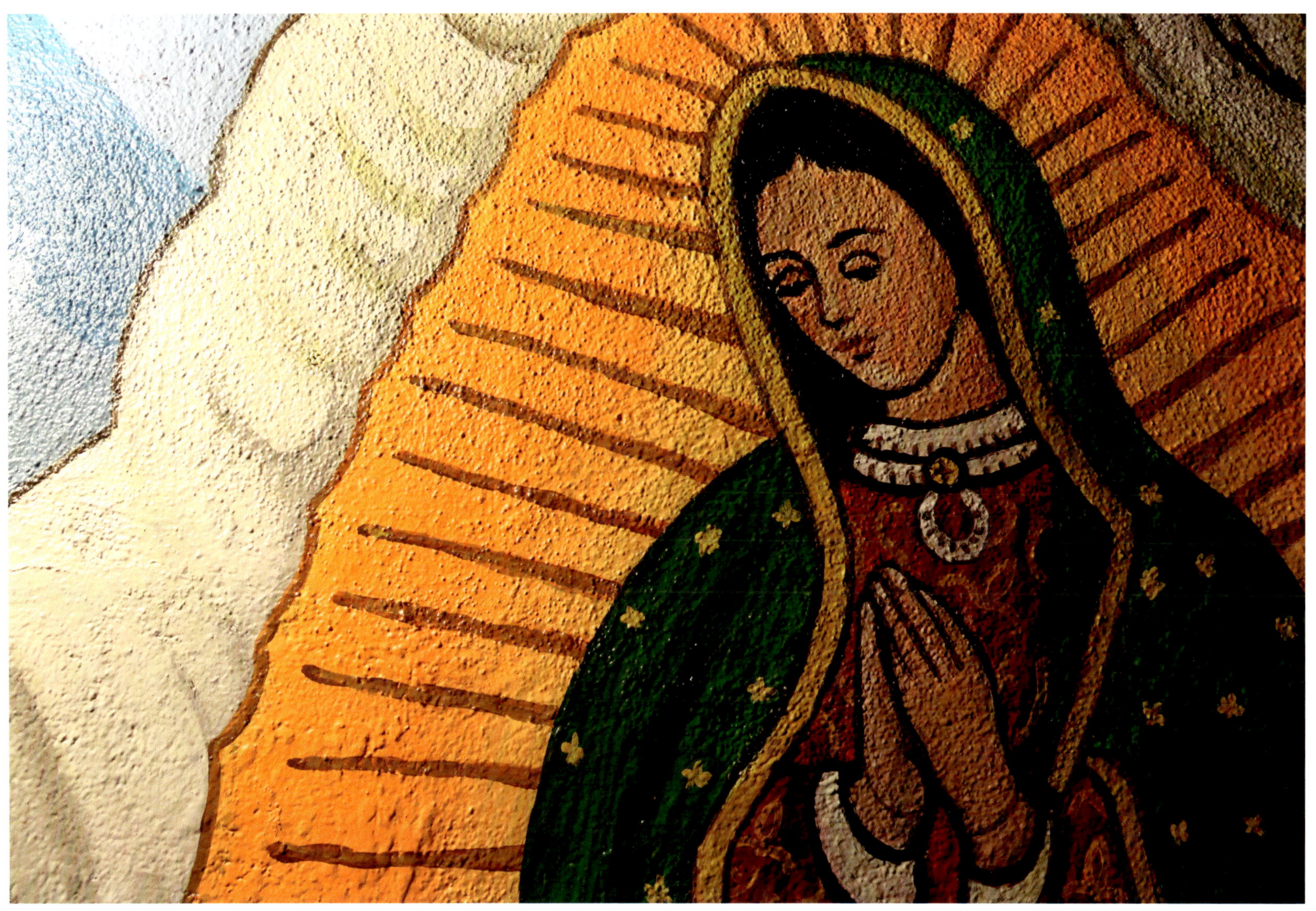

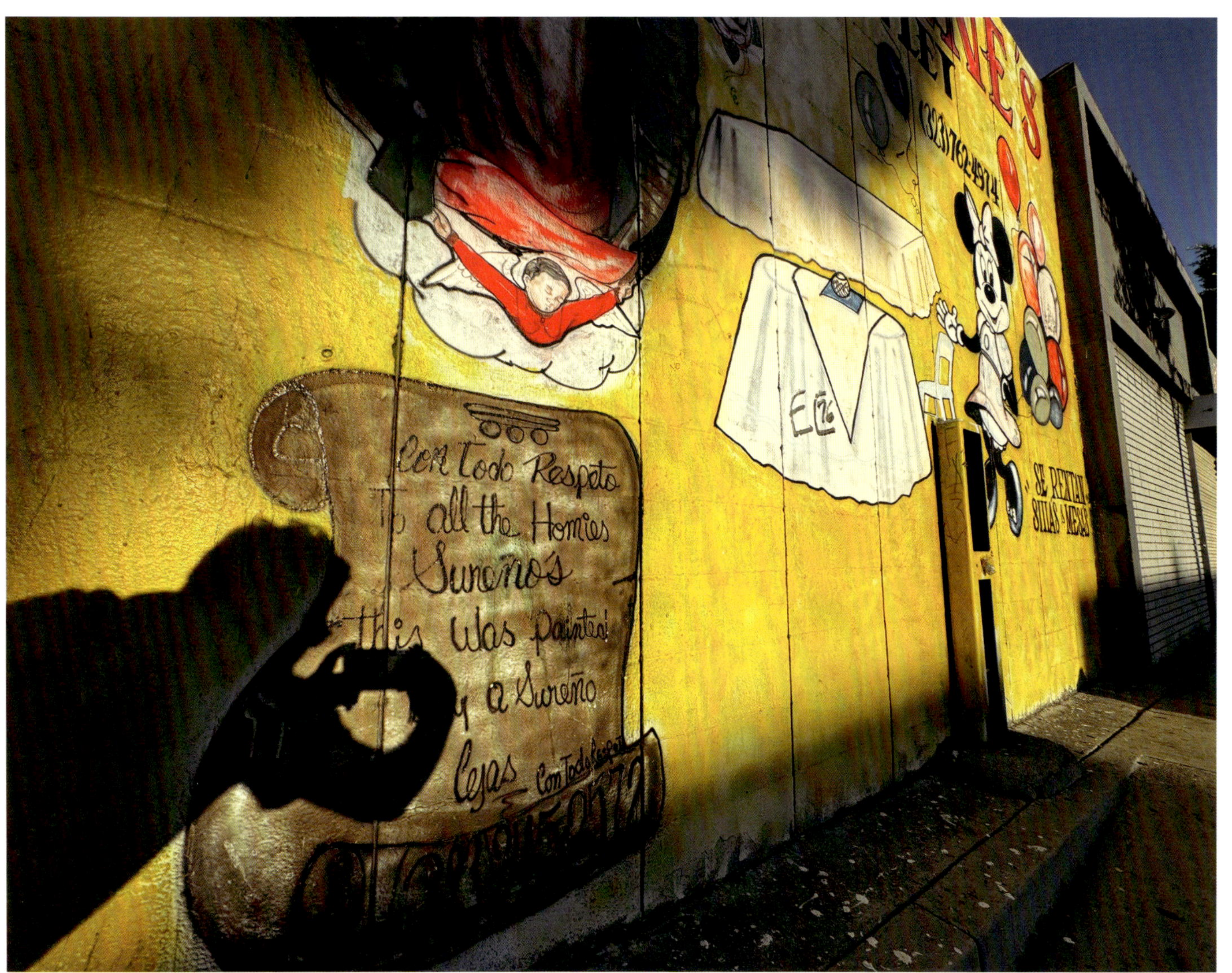
Con Todo Respeto
all the Homies
Sureño's
Was painted
a Sureño
Lejas
Con Todo Respeto
SE RENTAN
SILLAS Y MESAS

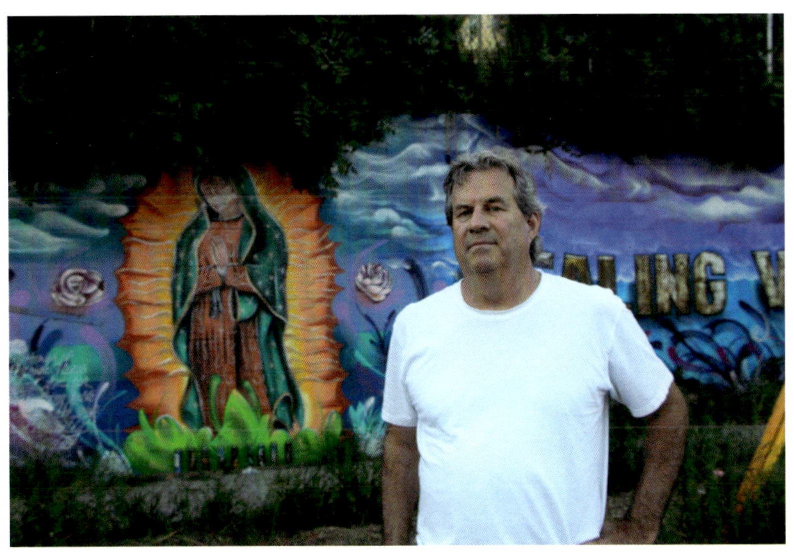

ABOUT THE AUTHOR

Sam Quinones is a Los Angeles-based independent journalist, who worked for ten years in Mexico (1994–2004), where he wrote the first two of his five books of narrative nonfiction. In 2004, he returned to Los Angeles where he worked for another ten years as a reporter for the *Los Angeles Times*. *Our Lady of the Angels* is his first book of photojournalism.

SOBRE EL AUTOR

Sam Quinones es un periodista independiente radicado en Los Ángeles, quien trabajó por diez años en México (1994–2004), donde escribió los primeros dos de sus ahora cinco libros de no-ficción narrativa. El regresó a Los Ángeles, donde trabajó por otros diez años como reportero para el Los Angeles Times. Nuestra Señora de Los Ángeles *es su primer libro de fotoperiodismo.*

samquinones.com

For photos, posters, a mural map, and more:
Para fotos, pósteres, mapa de los murales, y más:

samquinones.com/ourladyoftheangels

*

LOCATIONS

Cover: South Normandie Avenue at West 36th Street

Page 2: West 51st Street at Main Street

Page 4: West Avenue 37 at Figueroa Street

Page 6: Lorena Street at Siskiyou Street

Page 7: Duncan Avenue at Olympic Boulevard

Page 10: Worcester Avenue at Orange Grove Boulevard (Pasadena)

Page 11: 6th Street at Westlake Avenue

Page 15: 52nd Street at Avalon Boulevard (2011)

Page 16: Mozart Street at Workman Street (2021)

Page 17: Mozart Street at Workman Street (2016)

Page 18, left: Compton Avenue and Florence Avenue

Page 18, right: McKinley Avenue and Gage Avenue

Page 19: East 38th Street at South Avalon Boulevard

Page 20: Darwin Avenue at Eastlake Avenue

Page 21: West 42nd Place at South Vermont Avenue

Pages 22-23: Sichel Street at North Main Street

Pages 24-25: West Pico Boulevard at South Catalina Street

Page 26, left: North Avenue 52 and York Boulevard

Page 26, right: Drucker Street and North Eastern Avenue

Page 27: San Pedro Street and 33rd Street

Page 28: East First Street and North Boyle Avenue (Mariachi Plaza)

Page 30: Barbee Street at North Mission Road

Page 31: Barbee Street at North Mission Road

Page 32: Hooper Avenue and East 23rd Street

Page 33: Virgil Avenue at Burns Avenue

Pages 34-35: East Sixth Street at South Bonnie Beach Place

Page 36: Boulder Street at North Fickett Street

Page 37: Pomeroy Street at Tremont Street

Page 39: Barbee Street at North Mission Road

Page 40: East 54th Street and South Central Avenue

Page 41: Martin Luther King Boulevard at Broadway Place

Page 42, left: Avalon Boulevard and East 84th Street

Page 42, right: Unknown

Page 43, left: Bandera Street at Firestone Boulevard

Page 43, right: North Avenue 58 at Figueroa Street

Page 44: North Avenue 52 and York Boulevard

Page 45: North Avenue 52 and Monte Vista Street

Pages 46-47: South Avalon Boulevard at East 59th Place

Page 48: Hooper Avenue at 60th Street

Page 49: Sichel Street at North Main Street

Page 51: East 27th Street at South San Pedro Street

Pages 52-53: Santa Fe Street at Walter Street

Page 54: Maple Street at East 32nd Street

Page 56: Fickett Street and East Cesar Chavez Avenue

Page 57: Worcester Avenue at Orange Grove Boulevard (Pasadena)

Page 58: Lancaster Avenue at Murchison Street (Ramona Gardens)

Page 59: North Cummings Street at Marengo Street

Page 60: San Pedro Street and East 24th Street

Page 62: Eastlake Avenue and Darwin Avenue

Page 63: West 41st Street and South Broadway

Page 64: Holmes Avenue and East Florence Avenue

Page 66: Hooper Avenue at East Vernon Avenue

Page 67: West 51st Street at Main Street

Page 68: South Rowan Street at Princeton Street

Page 69: Maycrest Avenue at North Huntington Drive

Page 71: South Avalon Boulevard at East 43rd Place

Page 72: North Hazard Avenue at Hammel Street

Page 73: Griffith Avenue at East 32nd Street

Pages 74-75: East 35th Street at South Main Street

Page 76: Central Avenue and East 69th Street

Page 79: East 36th Street and San Pedro Street

Page 81: South Lorena Street at Beswick Street

Page 82: Mozart Street at Daly Street

Page 83: East 71st Street and South Avalon Boulevard

Page 84: South Breed Street at Whittier Boulevard

Page 85: North Avenue 58 at Figueroa Street

Page 86: West Pico Boulevard at South Catalina Street

Page 87: South Central Avenue at East 32nd Street

Page 88-89: 52nd Street at Avalon Boulevard (2021)

Page 90: West 40th Street at Broadway Place

Page 93a: Cesar Chavez Avenue

Page 93b: Central Avenue and 41st Street

Page 94: Broadway Place and West 40th Street

Page 96: Maple Street at East 32nd Street

Page 97: Fickett Street at Wabash Avenue

Page 99: Lorena Street at Beswick Street

Page 100: Hooper Street at East 50th Street

Page 103: East 36th Street at South San Pedro Street

Page 104: Maple Street at East 32nd Street

Page 109: Compton Avenue and East 78th Street

Page 110: Sierra Street at Mercury Avenue

OUR LADY OF THE ANGELS

The Virgin of Guadalupe on the Walls of Los Angeles

By Sam Quinones

Design by Thunderwing, with cross illustration by Adam Siegel

10 9 8 7 6 5 4 3 2 1
ISBN-13 978-1-62640-040-5 (print edition)
ISBN-13 978-1-62640-060-3 (e-pub edition)

Library of Congress Cataloging-in-Publication Data is available

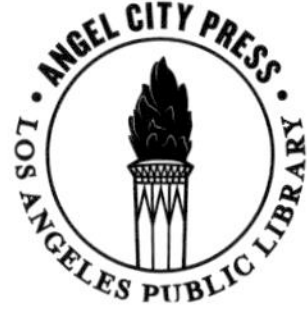

Published by Angel City Press at Los Angeles Public Library
www.angelcitypress.com

Printed in Canada